# Managing for Mission Assurance in the Face of Advanced Cyber Threats

DON SNYDER, LAUREN A. MAYER, MYRON HURA, SUZANNE GENC,
COLBY PEYTON STEINER, LAURA WERBER, KATHRYN O'CONNOR,
KEITH GIERLACK, PAUL DREYER, BERNARD FOX

Prepared for the Department of the Air Force
Approved for public release; distribution unlimited

RAND PROJECT AIR FORCE

For more information on this publication, visit **www.rand.org/t/RR4198**.

**About RAND**

The RAND Corporation is a research organization that develops solutions to public policy challenges to help make communities throughout the world safer and more secure, healthier and more prosperous. RAND is nonprofit, nonpartisan, and committed to the public interest. To learn more about RAND, visit www.rand.org.

**Research Integrity**

Our mission to help improve policy and decisionmaking through research and analysis is enabled through our core values of quality and objectivity and our unwavering commitment to the highest level of integrity and ethical behavior. To help ensure our research and analysis are rigorous, objective, and nonpartisan, we subject our research publications to a robust and exacting quality-assurance process; avoid both the appearance and reality of financial and other conflicts of interest through staff training, project screening, and a policy of mandatory disclosure; and pursue transparency in our research engagements through our commitment to the open publication of our research findings and recommendations, disclosure of the source of funding of published research, and policies to ensure intellectual independence. For more information, visit www.rand.org/about/principles.

RAND's publications do not necessarily reflect the opinions of its research clients and sponsors.

Published by the RAND Corporation, Santa Monica, Calif.
© 2021 RAND Corporation
**RAND®** is a registered trademark.

Library of Congress Cataloging-in-Publication Data is available for this publication.

ISBN: 978-1-9774-0614-9

*Cover design: Rick Penn-Kraus.*

# Preface

The objective of the project documented here was to examine how cybersecurity might be better managed at the enterprise level in the U.S. Air Force, including the allocation of roles and responsibilities for the central tasks for securing cyberspace and ensuring Air Force missions despite attacks through cyberspace. This report should be of interest to all in the Air Force and to many other government agencies.

The research reported here was commissioned by the Air Force Chief Information Dominance and Chief Information Officer in the Office of the Secretary of the Air Force and conducted within the Resource Management Program of RAND Project AIR FORCE as part of a fiscal year 2018 project, "Organizational Roles in Cyberspace Mission Assurance."

## RAND Project AIR FORCE

RAND Project AIR FORCE (PAF), a division of the RAND Corporation, is the U.S. Air Force's federally funded research and development center for studies and analyses. PAF provides the Air Force with independent analyses of policy alternatives affecting the development, employment, combat readiness, and support of current and future air, space, and cyber forces. Research is conducted in four programs: Force Modernization and Employment; Manpower, Personnel, and Training; Resource Management; and Strategy and Doctrine. The research reported here was prepared under contract FA7014-16-D-1000.

Additional information about PAF is available on our website:
http://www.rand.org/paf

This report documents work originally shared with the U.S. Air Force on September 26, 2018. The draft report, issued on September 26, 2018, was reviewed by formal peer reviewers and U.S. Air Force subject-matter experts.

# Contents

# Figures and Table

## Figures

## Table

# Summary

The organizational structure of the U.S. Air Force, while constantly evolving over time, was not designed to meet current threats through cyberspace. These nonkinetic threats are unique in this setting; they are highly dynamic, complex, and ubiquitous in time and space. Cybersecurity activities throughout the Air Force have organically organized themselves to be somewhat fractionated,[1] with blurred lines of authority and no overall coordinating mechanism to ensure that all related cybersecurity activities are identified, tasked, and implemented and act in concert to achieve enterprise objectives.

In this report, we develop the foundation for better managing cybersecurity at the enterprise level aimed at mission assurance in the Air Force. This structure includes guidance on the allocation of roles and responsibilities for cybersecurity tasks and mechanisms to create a cohesive initiative in which each individual and organization is working toward a common goal.

Our principal recommendation is that the Air Force adopt a concise objective for cybersecurity that is agnostic of how it is to be achieved, focuses on mission outcomes, and communicates the roles that all individuals and organizations must play. We offer the objective *to ensure that the Air Force maintains the advantage over adversaries in cyberspace and that all Air Force missions can be accomplished despite threats through cyberspace.*

To achieve that objective, the policy should follow with a concise strategy to direct and coordinate its various organizations. Excluding offensive operations, we proffer the following enterprisewide strategy for securing cyberspace:

- *to limit adversary advantage from the exfiltration of data, and*
- *to have the ability to operate through a cyberattack,*
  - *with an acceptable degradation of mission capability*
  - *for an acceptable duration of time.*

Following this strategy, perhaps issued by the Secretary of the Air Force as a revision of Air Force Policy Directive 17-1 and directed to all Air Force members, we further recommend that the policy, using a strategies-to-tasks framework, articulate the full range of integrated activities that need to be done to achieve this objective across the Air Force and assign the tasks to appropriate organizations.

The treatment of cybersecurity activities should employ a balance of cyber defensive measures and cyber resiliency measures (of systems and missions) and employ a balance of

---

[1] We use the term *cybersecurity* in this report to refer to all activities to thwart an adversary's objectives in cyber operations, including both defensive measures and those that make systems and missions resilient to adversary cyber operations. We exclude offensive actions.

enterprise networks and cyber-physical systems.[2] And it should clearly indicate that all individuals and organizations play a role in cybersecurity and that failure to perform that role effectively could be decisive.

Regarding roles and missions, we address three specific areas that pose particular challenges for cybersecurity:

- How should the roles and responsibilities for cybersecurity risk assessment be managed in the Air Force?
- Should the provision of information technology (IT) network services and the cybersecurity of those networks be managed together or separately?
- How should preparatory and operational cybersecurity activities be apportioned?

While some risk assessment activities are preparatory, such as those related to identifying system vulnerabilities and monitoring compliance, others must occur in reaction to crises, such as the risk assessments to assess vulnerabilities, mission impact, and tactical intelligence information in real time to respond to adversarial actions in cyberspace. We refer to the former as *strategic risk assessment* and to the latter as *tactical risk assessment*.

Assigning these two tasks, with widely different timescales, to the same organization can be problematic. The type of organizational structure that more efficiently manages quick response tasks (i.e., one that is decentralized into subunits, with a flatter hierarchy) differs from one that can better and more economically manage longer term, deliberative tasks. Furthermore, prioritization of short- and long-term risks within the same organization is bound to face competing demands, possibly resulting in one type being the focus over another. At the same time, divorcing tactical and strategic risk assessment for a given system or mission creates a seam in oversight and makes inconsistent assessments likely. Currently, authorities for these two types of risk are not clearly distinguished. Authorizing officials implicitly have authorities for both, but policies and processes that authorizing officials follow are designed for strategic risk assessment.

One way to resolve some of these challenges is to change policy so that tactical risk assessment and decisionmaking for cyber risk acceptance is assigned to operational authorities responsible for incident response. To mitigate creating an inconsistency between tactical and strategic risk assessment, the policy should state that the relevant authorizing official be consulted.

For strategic risk assessment, further difficulties exist in properly apportioning roles and responsibilities because (1) there are overlapping authorities for the program offices, the operational community, and the authorizing official (acting on behalf of the chief information officer); (2) policies designed for the cybersecurity of enterprise networks are sometimes ill-

---

[2] *Cyber-physical systems* "are engineered systems that are built from, and depend upon, the seamless integration of computation and physical components" (National Science Foundation, "Cyber-Physical Systems (CPS)," webpage, 2019). Examples include aircraft flight controls, avionics, and industrial control systems.

suited for cyber-physical systems; and (3) the risk management framework places undue emphasis on systems over missions. To partially redress these issues, we propose a realignment of the authorizing officials' roles for weapon systems such that the risk assessment and acceptance process for systems is placed on an equal footing with missions.

At the center of the proposal is that system and operational (mission) risk be assessed independently by equally resourced entities that are mutual peers. The system risk assessment would be done as it is currently, but the position would now be called *system risk assessor* (SRA). This individual would represent the concerns of the program office. Mirroring the SRA would be an *operational risk assessor*, a newly created position on par with the SRA. The authorizing official would take the system and operational risk assessments provided by the appropriate SRAs and operational risk assessors and decide what risks to accept. The boundaries of jurisdiction of authorizing officials would be mission boundaries. To facilitate cybersecurity actions, the authorizing official would be given a budget to allocate for cybersecurity. To carry out these extended duties, the authorizing official would need to be dedicated to this one job and be equipped with an appropriate staff.

Currently, the Air Force intertwines the provisioning of IT services with the cybersecurity of its networks (information security [InfoSec]), and the corresponding career fields are not clearly distinguished. In contrast, the commercial sector nearly always assigns these two task groupings to distinct organizations, whose personnel follow separate career tracks because of fundamental differences in their activities. The inherent unpredictability and uncertainty of the InfoSec environment requires its personnel to need more autonomy in decisionmaking. Furthermore, the increased responsiveness requirements of the InfoSec environment are better managed in a decentralized department, which can adapt to changes more quickly because it has greater user control; easier access to data; the ability to meet the needs of individual units; and access to the best local, relevant knowledge. In many companies, the InfoSec function is tightly integrated into the overall corporate risk management process, and decisions about security posture and investments are made from a business risk perspective, not an IT perspective. Each of these distinctions suggests that these two task groupings be managed by separate organizations.

A number of cybersecurity activities are preparatory, such as reducing the exposure of systems, building robust mission and system architectures, training personnel in sound cyber hygiene, assessing the strategic risk of a system or mission to a specific attack type, and planning and rehearsing ways to continue a mission in the event of a cyberattack. Others are more operational, such as those associated with detecting and responding to adversary cyber operations. The nature of the latter activities is less deliberate and more akin to crisis management. The first set of activities includes those a service typically does in its roles of organizing, training, and equipping forces to present to combatant commanders. The second set of activities more resembles activities that a service component command provides for a combatant commander.

With the exception of cyber threat analysis, most preparatory and operational activities are not currently distinctly separated in the Air Force. For risk assessment and acceptance, no explicit distinction is made between the strategic and tactical settings. For incident response, duties for the enterprise networks are assigned to units in the 16th Air Force. As argued for management of risk assessment and enterprise networks, assigning preparatory and operational duties to the same organization presents challenges.

Separating these two task groupings in the Air Force organization can have distinct advantages. Separation is useful to avoid conflicting demands (e.g., between short- and long-term objectives). It is also useful because organizations performing fast, complex operations tend to be decentralized, while those performing more-deliberate tasks that are less complex tend to centralize. Decentralization pushes decisions to lower levels in the organization, which tends to decrease decision time, increase flexibility, and place decisions closer to the locus of relevant information. Coordination of effort is achieved through strong horizontal coordination mechanisms. Centralization, on the other hand, facilitates the establishment of codified policies to coordinate effort and make decisions with an enterprise view.

Separating preparatory and operational activities, though, can be done without placing them in two separate organizations. A single organization can have mixed structures to accommodate the differing needs of each subdivision.

Air Force members will need to make some decisions in cybersecurity that will not be codified in policy. To handle these situations effectively, personnel will need to live in an appropriate cyber culture. The current culture is lacking, and leaders will need to be the vanguards in changing it. Leaders need to define a culture that, at minimum, includes the following:

- a sense that there is conflict in cyberspace between the United States and others that is ubiquitous in time and space
- a sense that operations in cyberspace might be decisive in warfare
- an understanding that all airmen, civilians, and contractors play a role in cybersecurity
- a realization that nothing can be completely secure in cyberspace, which leads personnel to have a sense of their responsibility to carry on their mission(s) in the face of an attack through cyberspace
- a sense that connecting one system to another (or to a network) carries potential risks
- a sense of obligation to report anomalies in data, nonnominal procedures, and potential cyber incidents.

The burden of changing this culture lies with leaders. Their actions will be more important than any words. Key actions would include paying attention to these cybersecurity matters; actively monitoring them; and making them true priorities consistently over time, including prioritizing them in the budget. The more passionate leaders are about these issues, the more it will help change the culture. Sanctions and rewards for individuals and units will bolster that message. To form a shared sense of reality, a common vocabulary that binds the Air Force together in this common, integrated activity rather than isolate cybersecurity to specialists will also reinforce these messages.

These changes alone will not solve cybersecurity in the Air Force. But without clear direction at the enterprise level that identifies the full range of tasks needed for cybersecurity and apportions and coordinates them well, even the well-executed actions of individuals and organizations risk being for naught if they leave gaps in their efforts and work in an uncoordinated way.

# Acknowledgments

We thank Pete Kim for initially sponsoring this work and Col William (Data) Bryant for all his assistance in carrying out the research. Rowayne (Wayne) Schatz, Jr., kindly continued the sponsorship of this work after the departure of the originating sponsor, and Col John (Mace) Moesner supported our work in the latter months. In the course of this research, a number of individuals, too numerous to cite individually, shared their insights into the management of cybersecurity. We especially thank Danny Holtzman and Dennis Miller for many stimulating discussions over the course of years.

At RAND, we are grateful to Lt Gen (retired) Robert Elder, Jr for several stimulating discussions and a formal review of the document. We also thank Jim Powers for reviewing an early draft of this report. Additional formal reviews by Caolionn O'Connell and Carra Sims improved the report.

That we received help and insights from those acknowledged above should not be taken to imply that they concur with the views expressed in this report. We alone are responsible for the content, including any errors or oversights.

# Abbreviations

| | |
|---|---|
| AFI | Air Force Instruction |
| AFNET | Air Force Network |
| AFNET-S | Air Force Network–Secure |
| AFPD | Air Force Policy Directive |
| CIO | chief information officer |
| CNSSI | Committee on National Security Systems Instruction |
| DoD | Department of Defense |
| InfoSec | information security |
| IT | information technology |
| OODA | observe, orient, decide, and act |
| ORA | operational risk assessor |
| SAF/CIO A6 | Chief, Information Dominance and Chief Information Officer |
| SRA | system risk assessor |
| USB | universal serial bus |
| U.S.C. | U.S. Code |

# 1. Framing the Problem

The Internet protocols and the programs built upon them were designed for an honest, cooperative and well-meaning community of trusted parties. That is not remotely what today's Internet is like, so on a variety of fronts, we are playing catch-up on information security and authentication.

—Brian W. Kernighan[1]

This is the root paradox of security in our times: those nations that are most adept at harnessing cyberspace to achieve economic, social, even military gains are also the ones most vulnerable to threats propagating through it.

—Lucas Kello[2]

## Introduction

In this report, we explore how to manage cybersecurity in the U.S. Air Force at the enterprise level. As we argue throughout, current management is somewhat fractionated, leading to sometimes well-executed—but uncoordinated—actions in different organizations. Some important tasks are not being done. And since some tasks can be interpreted as having been assigned to more than one organization, different organizations sometimes conflict on the bounds of authority. More-coordinated cybersecurity management would enhance overall Air Force mission readiness in the face of threats through cyberspace.

Before proceeding further, we need to be clear on what we mean by *cybersecurity*. Within the Department of Defense (DoD), the term is used somewhat differently in different contexts. There is a dimension of securing cyberspace that involves defensive measures. The goal of defensive measures is to secure data and the control of processes. Examples of these measures include denying access to unauthorized actors, administering counterintelligence activities against insider threats, and placing security controls on devices. Some use the term *cybersecurity* in the restricted sense, to refer only to these kinds of actions. A second dimension of securing cyberspace involves being able to absorb an attack through cyberspace, recover adequately from it, or both. The goal of this dimension is mission assurance. In some circles, the term *cyber resiliency* is used to describe these kinds of actions. Both these dimensions—defense and resiliency—are important. For our purposes, both are complementary dimensions of a unified effort and should not be viewed as independent activities. For this reason, and for brevity, we use the single term *cybersecurity* to express that unified effort of defensive and resilient measures.

---

[1] Brian W. Kernighan, *Understanding the Digital World: What You Need to Know About Computers, the Internet, Privacy, and Security*, Princeton, N.J.: Princeton University Press, 2017, p. 161.

[2] Lucas Kello, *The Virtual Weapon and International Order*, New Haven, Conn.: Yale University Press, 2017, p. 256.

When a distinction is needed, we call the two components of cybersecurity *cyber defensive measures* and *cyber resiliency*.

## Methodology

### Scope

We bound the discussion in this report to cybersecurity activities in systems under U.S. control. This constraint excludes activities that directly affect an adversary's capabilities by, for example, using a kinetic weapon, offensive cyber operations, or any other means to target an adversary asset being used to exploit or attack the Air Force, or disrupt an adversary's infrastructure, or any other means of directly diminishing an adversary's capabilities. These options are part of the full spectrum of cybersecurity, but we focus in this report on what the roles and responsibilities are for managing the elements of cybersecurity under U.S. control across the Air Force and how these should be allocated and coordinated among its various organizations.

This report does not assess or recommend specific technical solutions for cyber defensive measures. Neither does it propose procedures to ensure mission resiliency in the face of adversarial cyber operations. There are, of course, needs for continual research into new ways to counter cyber threats. Some additional solutions are still needed for existing threats, and the threats continue to evolve, requiring adaptation. But many well-known remedies are not being effectively and consistently employed. Existing patches for known vulnerabilities are not installed. Budgets do not allocate resources to address known cyber risks. Personnel across the Air Force are not adequately trained to counter the cyber threat. Poor practices of operators expose systems to malicious actors. Commanders do not fully prepare to have resilient operations in the event of a cyberattack, and so on. How can cybersecurity be managed such that these known issues can be effectively addressed in a coordinated fashion to achieve maximal results?

The Air Force organizes for the full range of training, equipping, and supplying forces to combatant commanders. Cybersecurity is just one of its responsibilities. For the most part, cybersecurity roles and responsibilities must be distributed across the existing organizational design. Most of our attention in this report will be on the broader activities that must be done to secure cyberspace, how those activities should be grouped together, and the desired attributes of organizations that might do these grouped activities. That is, what are the qualities of an organization that should do these activities? At times, the assignment of which organization should take certain roles and responsibilities will be clear and uncontroversial. At other times, certain roles and responsibilities might be assigned to more than one organization. In these cases, we will describe the pros and cons of various organizations taking on these assignments.

*Analytical Approach*

Our team examined law relevant to cybersecurity and Air Force organizational structure, as well as policies for cybersecurity at the DoD and Air Force levels. This examination was systematic at the level of Air Force issuances at the Air Staff level. Organizational structure in the Air Force constantly evolves. Although organizational units and reporting lines pertinent to cybersecurity changed during the course of this research, we examined the existing organizational roles and responsibilities throughout the Air Force for cybersecurity.

Extensive informal, unstructured interviews across the Air Force form an important foundation for much of the discussion in this report. We met with personnel at most levels in the hierarchy in the Air Force. We met with key organizations that are dedicated in various ways to cybersecurity, including the staff of the Chief, Information Dominance and Chief Information Officer (SAF/CIO A6), the 16th Air Force, the Cyber Resiliency Office for Weapons Systems, members of the intelligence community, members of the acquisition community, and cybersecurity personnel in the field.

We have also drawn from a number of meetings with individuals and organizations in the operational major commands who do not do cybersecurity as a primary part of their functions. These included operators, maintainers, and logisticians and were aimed at understanding how they perceived their roles in cybersecurity and what guidance they followed from leadership and policies. These interviews were supplemented by less extensive interviews of comparable personnel and organizations in the Navy and Army. The goal was to discover possible solutions that might be adapted to the Air Force or ones to avoid.

And we have drawn from an extensive review of cyber operations, some extracted from a review of the literature and some from extensive discussions with practitioners.

The overall structure of our analytical approach is guided by research in organizational design.[3] A strong organizational design includes both organizational structure and other design elements to best achieve an organization's mission.[4] To shape the management of cybersecurity across all members of the Air Force (or any organization), an organizational design approach suggests three central factors: (1) defining shared common goals of the Air Force for cybersecurity, (2) dividing the goals into tasks and assigning the tasks to organizations and

---

[3] Henry Mintzberg, *The Structuring of Organizations: A Synthesis of Research*, Englewood Cliffs, N.J.: Prentice-Hall, 1979; Dan R. Dalton, William D. Todor, Michael J. Spendolini, Gordon J. Fielding, and Lyman W. Porter, "Organization Structure and Performance: A Critical Review," *Academy of Management Review*, Vol. 5, No. 1, January 1980; Arnoldo C. Hax and Nicolas S. Majluf, "Organizational Design: A Survey and an Approach," *Operations Research*, Vol. 29, No. 3, May–June 1981; Richard M. Burton, Børge Obel, and Dorthe Døjbak Håkonsson, Organizational Design: A Step-by-Step Approach, 3rd ed., Cambridge University Press, 2015.

[4] Don Snyder, Bernard Fox, Kristin F. Lynch, Raymond E. Conley, John A. Ausink, Laura Werber, William Shelton, Sarah A. Nowak, Michael R. Thirtle, and Albert A. Robbert, *Assessment of the Air Force Materiel Command Reorganization: Report for Congress*, Santa Monica, Calif.: RAND Corporation, RR-389-AF, 2013, p. 24.

individuals,[5] and (3) coordinating the individual tasks to ensure that the sum of the divided labor yields the desired goal.

In addition to insights from organizational design, we draw on economic literature on the assignment of decision rights and the cognitive science literature on decisionmaking. We also compare the current and proposed organizational designs for cybersecurity in the Air Force with other organizations, including practices in industry and in other services. We extend these comparisons to how similar problems are tackled, specifically in how safety is managed, which we argue has some relevant similarities with cybersecurity.[6]

---

[5] In this report, we follow a strategies-to-tasks framework for the cybersecurity goal; see Glenn A. Kent, *Concepts of Operations: A More Coherent Framework for Defense Planning*, Santa Monica, Calif.: RAND Corporation, N-2026-AF, 1983; Glenn A. Kent, *A Framework for Defense Planning*, Santa Monica, Calif.: RAND Corporation, R-3721-AF/OSD, 1989; David E. Thaler, *Strategies to Tasks: A Framework for Linking Means and Ends*, Santa Monica, Calif.: RAND Corporation, MR-300-AF, 1993; and Glenn A. Kent, with David Ochmanek, Michael Spirtas, and Bruce R. Pirnie, *Thinking About America's Defense: An Analytical Memoir*, Santa Monica, Calif.: RAND Corporation, OP-223-AF, 2008, pp. 115–121.

[6] See also Don Snyder, James D. Powers, Elizabeth Bodine-Baron, Bernard Fox, Lauren Kendrick, and Michael H. Powell, *Improving the Cybersecurity of U.S. Air Force Military Systems Throughout Their Life Cycles*, Santa Monica, Calif.: RAND Corporation, RR-1007-AF, 2015, p. 15.

# 2. Specifying the Objective, Strategy, and Tasks

> A good strategy doesn't just draw on existing strength; it creates strength through the coherence of its design. Most organizations of any size don't do this. Rather, they pursue multiple objectives that are unconnected with one another or, worse, that conflict with one another.
>
> —Richard P. Rumelt[1]

> Organizations expand their comprehension of history by making experience richer, by considering multiple interpretations of experience, by using experience to discover and modify their preferences, and by simulating near-events and hypothetical histories. They try to learn from samples of one or fewer.
>
> —James G. March, Lee S. Sproull, and Michal Tamuz[2]

To be effective and efficient, an enterprise needs a clear, coherent objective. Ideally, each organizational unit in the enterprise then carries out distinct assigned tasks to meet this objective. To ensure completeness, the tasks must be reasonably comprehensive. It is further desirable for the tasks and objective to be linked in a hierarchy such that, looking downward in the hierarchy, it can be seen how the objective is to be done via distinct tasks assigned to one or more organizational units; looking upward in the hierarchy, each task can be rationalized by what role it plays in achieving the overall objective. That role is documented by an audit trail upward through the hierarchy that links tasks to the overall objective. The strategies-to-tasks framework was designed for this purpose.[3]

The strategies-to-tasks framework provides an end-to-end structure for linking systems to the national objectives they support. It was developed to assist in force planning and to develop and rationalize force structure investments. The strategies-to-tasks framework decomposes objectives to strategies, strategies to campaign objectives, campaign objectives to operational objectives, operational objectives to operational tasks, and operational tasks to weapon systems. By linking systems to specific strategies through an audit trail upward in a hierarchical decomposition, each system can be justified by how it contributes to national objectives, and it can be seen how national objectives can be met given a force structure and concepts of operations by tracing the links downward.

In this chapter, we follow a strategies-to-tasks framework for defining the higher-level tasks for Air Force cybersecurity. We borrow key elements of this framework, chief among them the

---

[1] Richard P. Rumelt, *Good Strategy, Bad Strategy: The Difference and Why It Matters*, New York: Crown Business, 2011, p. 9.

[2] James G. March, Lee S. Sproull, and Michal Tamuz, "Learning From Samples of One or Fewer," *Organization Science*, Vol. 2, No. 1, February 1991, p. 5.

[3] Kent, 1983; Kent, 1989; Thaler, 1993; Kent et al., 2008, pp. 115–121.

structure of decomposition from an objective, to a strategy, to tasks (the activities and means to carry out the strategy). We seek a relatively comprehensive decomposition at the highest levels in the hierarchy and clear linkages to a strategy. This approach serves two goals for cybersecurity: to ensure that the objective is adequately covered by the requisite activities and to rationalize those activities in terms of how they contribute to an enterprise cybersecurity objective.

## Objective

The first step is to state the objective. The objective is an Air Force–wide goal stating a desired outcome that is agnostic of how it is to be achieved. It does not specify systems to be used, concepts of operations, or any other means by which the goal is to be accomplished. As we discuss further in Chapter 2, Air Force policy currently lacks a well-specified objective for cybersecurity. We proffer that the objective of securing cyberspace in the Air Force is *to ensure that the Air Force maintains the advantage over adversaries in cyberspace and that all Air Force missions can be accomplished despite threats through cyberspace*. This objective makes the completion of Air Force missions the central focus of cybersecurity.

## Strategy

To achieve that objective, the Air Force needs a concise strategy to direct and coordinate its various organizations. The aforementioned policy shortcomings related to a cybersecurity objective have made it difficult for the Air Force to proffer a clear cybersecurity strategy. Excluding offensive operations, we suggest the following as the enterprisewide strategy for securing cyberspace:

- *to limit adversary advantage from the exfiltration of data,[4] and*
- *to have the ability to operate through a cyberattack,*
  - *with an acceptable degradation of mission capability*
  - *for an acceptable duration of time.*

Attacks through cyberspace include denying access to data, compromising the integrity of data, and using cyberspace to degrade a mission (e.g., by taking control of a system or inducing physical damage to a system that is critical to a mission). The strategy cannot be carried out by just the organizations and personnel currently dedicated to cybersecurity. *Every organization and individual in the Air Force has some responsibilities for carrying out this strategy.*

DoD Instruction (DoDI) 8500.01 comes close to expressing this concept:

---

[4] We use the term *exfiltration* to mean "[t]he unauthorized transfer of information from an information system" (Committee on National Security Systems Instruction [CNSSI] 4009, *Committee on National Security Systems (CNSS) Glossary*, Committee on National Security Systems, April 6, 2015).

a. The purpose of the Defense cybersecurity program is to ensure that IT [information technology] can be used in a way that allows mission owners and operators to have confidence in the confidentiality, integrity, and availability of IT and DoD information, and to make choices based on that confidence.

b. The Defense cybersecurity program supports DoD's vision of effective operations in cyberspace where:

(1) DoD missions and operations continue under any cyber situation or condition.

(2) The IT components of DoD weapons systems and other defense platforms perform as designed and adequately meet operational requirements.

(3) The DoD Information Enterprise collectively, consistently, and effectively acts in its own defense.

(4) DoD has ready access to its information and command and control channels, and its adversaries do not.

(5) The DoD Information Enterprise securely and seamlessly extends to mission partners. [5]

This statement falls short of a strategy in several ways. One drawback is that it distracts from the ubiquity of cybersecurity equities throughout the DoD by focusing so much on IT rather than the mission. It lacks brevity and direction relevant to the equities that all actors have with cybersecurity. And, most important, it fails to express an explicit need for thresholds for what constitutes unacceptable levels of data loss and unacceptable levels of atrophy in terms of degree and duration of mission degradation.[6] It is not possible to ensure that no data get exfiltrated and that all attacks can be prevented. The ambiguity due to absence of thresholds also limits the ability to measure performance and hold actors accountable.[7] *An understanding of these thresholds is a key part of cyber situational awareness and, therefore, a key part of a strategy for securing cyberspace.*

The object of the remainder of this report is to guide how to assign the roles and responsibilities for achieving our proposed cybersecurity strategy to the various Air Force organizations. In doing so, organizational mechanisms will be needed to ensure the sum of the efforts of all organizations achieve the desired integrated objective, which is the subject of the Chapter 3.

---

[5] Department of Defense Instruction 8500.01, *Cybersecurity*, Department of Defense, March 14, 2014.

[6] As we argue in subsequent chapters, Air Force Policy Directive (AFPD) 17-1 inherits these limitations (AFPD 17-1, *Cyberspace: Information Dominance Governance and Management*, Washington, D.C.: Department of the Air Force, April 12, 2016).

[7] See Don Snyder, Lauren A. Mayer, Guy Weichenberg, Danielle C. Tarraf, Bernard Fox, Myron Hura, Suzanne Genc, and Jonathan W. Welburn, *Measuring Cybersecurity and Cyber Resiliency*, Santa Monica, Calif.: RAND Corporation, RR-2703-AF, 2020.

## Tasks

Although deceptively simple, the cybersecurity strategy we proffer has a number of dimensions. Covering these dimensions requires even more tasks. Before we unpack this strategy and focus on some specific tasks, it is important to understand the full range that the cybersecurity strategy touches.

We emphasize again that, to ensure cybersecurity as we define it in Chapter 1, every organization and individual has roles and responsibilities. To be successful in cyberspace operations, an adversary needs to gain access to relevant systems and must know enough to create some effect that negatively affects an Air Force mission. The adversary has many options available to achieve each of these steps. As one example, to gain access to a system, an adversary might enter through the supply chain, through apertures to the system, to systems that connect to the target system, through an insider, and so on. Securing a mission, therefore, touches every part of the enterprise. Because of this reach, larger cultural shifts will be needed across the Air Force and its contractors, a topic we address at length in Chapter 5. The more integrated and cohesive the cybersecurity efforts, the more likely they are to be effective and the more likely the requisite cultural changes will occur.

The strategy for cybersecurity identifies the need to limit exfiltration and the effects of attack through cyberspace to acceptable levels. All efforts revolve around the nucleus of these two desiderata. As in all other facets of warfare, some attrition is expected, so the fulcrum of these efforts is an assessment of what constitutes an "acceptable" level of loss. A decision on risk tolerance emerges from a combination of risk assessment, what is critical to the mission, and what level of effort is needed to allay the impacts of the cyber insult. The strategy is not just defensive, but also one of planning and rehearsing how to carry on the mission despite any adversary cyber operations. Any organization or individual whose systems or missions use, process, or transmit data therefore plays an important role in cybersecurity, which is to say, all organizations and individuals.

We used the strategies-to-tasks framework to decompose the proposed cyber strategy into high-level tasks. We took as a departure point a view implicit in that strategy, which is that the objective is to thwart an adversary's actions (as opposed to listing all possible Air Force actions).[8] An adversary needs to be able to access a system of interest, know enough about it to achieve some effect, and possess the necessary capabilities to do so, and that effect needs to have a negative impact of some significance to the Air Force. Our example decomposition is based on our collective knowledge of cyber operations and Air Force missions.

The result is the illustrative division of tasks in Table 2.1. The left column of the table indicates three strategy groupings: those unique to exfiltration, those unique to cyberattack, and those common to both. The substrategy elements are larger, higher-level activities to reduce the

---

[8] See Snyder et al., 2020.

8

consequences of both exfiltration and cyberattack. The next column gives one more potential indenture of these direct activities. The far righthand column lists the major indirect, enabling activities.

**Table 2.1. Summary of Illustrative High-Level Strategies-to-Tasks Decomposition**

| Strategy Elements | Strategy Subelements | Direct, High-Level Tasks | Indirect, Enabling Tasks[a] |
|---|---|---|---|
| Limit the consequences of exfiltration | Identify critical data | • Identify data that reveal critical technologies<br>• Identify data that reveal susceptibilities and vulnerabilities<br>• Identify data that reveal Air Force operations | |
| Limit the consequences of exfiltration and ensure missions in spite of cyberattack | Look for susceptibilities and vulnerabilities | • Blue team examination of susceptibility to exfiltration or cyberattack<br>• Red team examination of susceptibility to exfiltration or cyberattack<br>• Hold personnel accountable for deliberate infractions | • Write doctrine and policies to codify practices in cybersecurity<br>• Hire, train, sustain, and retain cyber-aware workforce<br>• Define cybersecurity requirements<br>• Acquire cybersecurity systems and services and ensure all acquisition programs prioritize cybersecurity<br>• Prioritize cybersecurity activities, given resource constraints<br>• Budget for cybersecurity<br>• Conduct basic and applied research into cybersecurity |
| | Reduce exposure of systems | • Protect the supply chain<br>• Secure data pathways<br>• Protect against insider threats | |
| | Complicate the adversary's cyberoperations | • Change system configurations<br>• Employ deception | |
| | Understand the threat | • Tactical warning of exfiltration or cyberattack<br>• Strategic warning of exfiltration or cyberattack<br>• Attribution | |
| | Assess risk, cost, and benefit trade-offs for mitigation | • Assess risk<br>• Identify mitigations (materiel and nonmateriel)<br>• Analyze benefits of mitigations<br>• Estimate costs of mitigations<br>• Weigh risks, benefits, and costs to choose a course of action | |
| | Respond to incidents | • Establish a baseline for data integrity and system behavior<br>• Monitor for departures from baseline, access breaches, and data exfiltration or cyberattack<br>• Detect exfiltration or cyberattack<br>• Evaluate operational impact<br>• Restore to baseline<br>• Disseminate lessons learned | |
| Ensure missions in spite of cyberattack | Identify critical mission elements | • Understand mission architecture and dependencies on data, communications links, and systems<br>• Understand when mission elements' failure is critical to missions and duration | |
| | Identify critical systems and data | • Identify which systems are critical to which missions<br>• Identify which data and communications are most critical to which missions | |
| | Develop plans to ensure mission resiliency | • Identify and rehearse ways to restore data, or data systems<br>• Identify and rehearse ways to restore the mission in absence of restoring data or data systems | |

[a] Apply to all strategy elements.

9

*Direct Tasks*

We first address tasks that directly support the strategy. We break these down only to the highest levels of activities to illustrate the decomposition from strategy to the means to carry out that strategy. Each of these high-level tasks becomes a strategy for the next level down in the hierarchy, and so on. It is not possible to list all the activities down to the lowest levels in the hierarchy (organization). In fact, many tasks at the lowest levels can only be identified with local knowledge, and the needed activities will evolve over time as circumstances change. But at the higher levels we discuss here, the tasks are relatively stable.

### Limiting the Consequences of Exfiltration

The goal of this part of the strategy is to limit, to an acceptable level, the amount of information exfiltrated from Air Force systems and information about Air Force systems and missions. This immediately leads to a task of identifying what constitutes an acceptable level. Clearly, the factors to consider are those that negatively affect the Air Force because of the loss of information. Adversaries can use exfiltrated information in multiple ways. They can develop countermeasures to Air Force systems and tactics. They can gain situational awareness of operations and improve their strategies, for example, by examining logistics data. They can use stolen technological data to accelerate development and fielding of their own weapon systems, thereby accelerating obsolescence of Air Force systems. Understanding what data are most critical and therefore most important to guard against exfiltration requires evaluating these risks and balancing them with the resources needed to secure the associated data and the estimated benefits (effectiveness) of potential mitigations.

There is, of course, a formal process for performing such a risk assessment for a wide range of Air Force data: the security classification system. The classification system is used to determine how information is guarded and when to employ antitamper technologies. This risk analysis is biased toward information under the control of a program office and information about operations. Yet this risk assessment does not extend equally to all Air Force data. Combat support (logistics) data is one example. Security classification guides do not adequately address the risks of compilation of these data. With modern data analysis techniques and computing power, the compilation of combat support information, such as supply-chain activities and aircraft maintenance data, can greatly enhance an adversary's situational awareness and potentially place Air Force operations at risk. Nevertheless, these data are generally deemed unclassified because the risks of their disclosure are assessed in isolation. The need to assess the risks of these data being aggregated and analyzed has increased with increasing computer speeds and algorithms for analysis of patterns in large data sets.

### Ensuring Air Force Missions Despite an Attack

Cyberattacks can directly alter data, deny access to data, destroy data, interrupt the transmission of data, or assume control of systems. Indirect effects can lead to physical damage of systems and, if well targeted, impair mission execution. To keep mission impact to an acceptable level in the event of a cyberattack, there is a need for situational awareness of which mission elements are most critical and which systems, data, and communications links are most critical for supporting those mission elements. That information provides the necessary foundation for assessing risk. With that knowledge of risk, those responsible for missions— whether supporting such activities as supply-chain operations and aircraft maintenance or directly responsible for dropping bombs or launching missiles—are hindered in their efforts to plan and rehearse for how to operate in a cyber-contested environment.

### Ensuring Against Both Exfiltration and Cyberattack

Many activities serve to mitigate both exfiltration and cyberattack. The two vectors are related. Some adversarial exfiltration might be done as intelligence preparation for a later cyberattack. Activities that serve the dual role of mitigating both vectors include examining systems for susceptibilities and vulnerabilities, reducing the exposure of systems to attack, understanding the threat, assessing risks (and the benefits and costs of mitigating them), and responding to cyber incidents.

### *Enabling Tasks*

All the above direct actions need some degree of institutional support, which, in many cases, enables many or all of the direct actions. These include writing policy; hiring, training, sustaining, and retaining a workforce; defining cybersecurity requirements for systems and tactics, techniques, and procedures; acquiring systems and services (some specifically for cyber operations, all others with adequate cybersecurity); budgeting for (and prioritizing) all these activities in the Air Force program objective memorandum; and conducting basic and applied research into cybersecurity.

## Managing Cybersecurity

We broke down the strategy into smaller tasks in Table 2.1 and the preceding discussion for two purposes. The first is to guide the decisions that leaders make so that they all do their part for cybersecurity and that these individual efforts are sufficiently coherent and coordinated to accomplish the objective.[9] The second is to identify gaps, overlaps, lack of coordination, and misalignments in the management of cybersecurity. We discuss the latter topic in Chapter 3 and focus the rest of this chapter on the former.

---

[9] Throughout this chapter, the term *leader* will refer to any officer or civilian in a leadership position in the Air Force across all functional areas (e.g., logistics, intelligence, medical, life-cycle management). It is not restricted to the chain of command or to the operational or IT-side of the Air Force.

Figure 2.1 depicts the management of cybersecurity as a process control loop.[10] The objective and strategy (described above) guide management decisions, shown in the upper left of the figure. Following the loop clockwise, these decisions determine purposeful actions meant to positively alter the state of cybersecurity in the Air Force. Feedback informs the decisions that management makes, completing the loop. The feedback takes two forms: feedback on the state of cybersecurity (solid line in Figure 2.1) and feedback on compliance with the management-directed actions (broken line in Figure 2.1). The first measures how well cybersecurity is really being done; the latter measures how well policies are being implemented.

**Figure 2.1. Cybersecurity Management as a Process Control Loop**

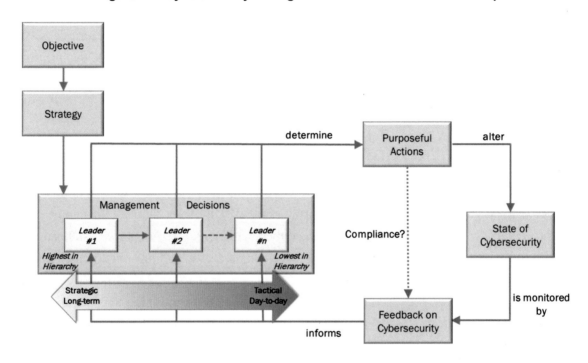

NOTE: Figure is modified from Snyder et al., 2015, Figure 1.2.

The feedback on the state of cybersecurity primarily informs decisionmaking. Since leaders at different levels in the Air Force hierarchy make different decisions, they need different feedback. Those at the highest levels need feedback to inform decisions toward the strategic end of the spectrum and, in general, longer-term matters. Those at the lower levels need feedback to inform decisions toward the tactical end of the spectrum and, in general, shorter-term matters. These distinctions are depicted in Figure 2.1 by separate branches in the feedback loop from the feedback to the various leadership levels in the hierarchy of management decisions.

---

[10] The model of management as a process control loop dates back at least as far as John D. Steinbruner, *The Cybernetic Theory of Decision*, Princeton, N.J.: Princeton University Press, 1974. The discussion in this section builds on Snyder et al., 2015, Ch. 1.

*Tracing Up to the Objective*

To see some of the benefits of a strategies-to-tasks perspective on cybersecurity, consider a leader somewhere in the middle of the hierarchy overseeing, say, some logistics function. That leader would be instructed by the objective and strategy and, with the help of policies that break down that strategy into activities, as illustrated in Table 2.1, the leader would see the specific roles and responsibilities that they have, as well as how the activities fit into a larger, coordinated set of activities that others have.

The leader would see the need to understand the criticality of data within their control. Of what value would that data be to an adversary, especially when combined with other data held at the same security level? What missions could be at risk? In the case of logistics, the leader might realize that, although held as unclassified and not explicitly treated in any security classification guide, the data could give the adversary considerable insight into the Air Force's air order of battle. For practical reasons, the data might be difficult to reclassify, but the leader would be better informed on the situational awareness of the adversary. If this insight were to be well communicated, the combatant command would be able to think through how to operate in this environment and what might be at risk.

The leader would understand the importance of identifying critical mission elements, the critical systems that support the mission elements, and the most critical data and communications links used in the mission. These insights would form the foundation for developing plans for how to continue operations in the face of a cyberattack. How would the mission be carried on if certain data were lost or corrupted? How would the mission be carried on if certain systems failed? The leader would be directed from above to maintain and rehearse these plans.

Finally, the leader would explicitly see the need for reducing the exposure of the systems under his or her purview. What role does the organization and its individuals play in shaping the exposure of the systems? Are poor practices, such as improper cyber hygiene, placing systems at risk? What are the potential consequences to the mission?

Leaders already do some of these activities. The framework guides leaders systematically through all the roles that they should embrace to have comprehensive, integrated cybersecurity.

*Tracing Down to the Tasks*

Each leader also has a responsibility to look down the strategies-to-tasks chain. To illustrate, we begin at the top of the Air Force hierarchy.

A central responsibility is to ensure that those lower in the hierarchy are doing all they should. Are there gaps in cybersecurity activities, and is any additional coordination needed? The framework provides a checklist of the means of carrying out the strategy. That checklist is a guide for what to monitor in the organization for situational awareness of how well cybersecurity is being performed.[11]

A second responsibility is to ensure that those lower in the hierarchy have the appropriate resources to carry out their responsibilities. Those resources include manpower, funding, and the training and technical support to perform such activities as reducing the exposure of a system or assessing risk.

There are a remarkable number of ways in which a system (and the systems with which it is connected) can be placed at risk. Many of these are subtle and highly technical. They require considerable expertise to manage, expertise that lies at lower levels in the Air Force, close to the locus of knowledge. The breakdown of the strategy to tasks needs to lead lower levels in the Air Force to the right areas, but finding the exact details to manage must be identified at the lower levels (the level where the locus of knowledge lies).

One example is connecting a device to a universal serial bus (USB) port. At the time of this writing, the dangers of the use of thumb drives with a USB port are widely known, and thumb drives are therefore generally banned in the DoD because of these risks. But the USB ports are often still present in devices. Violations of the policy are, therefore, still possible. Further, the dangers are not restricted to thumb drives. Risks extend to mice, keyboards, and other peripherals that use the USB interface, risks that are not as widely discussed.[12]

Another subtle set of threat vectors is a class of methods called *side-channel attacks*. These attacks intercept information from electronic emissions, changes in power consumption, vibrations, and other indirect means.[13] Reducing the exposure of systems to maintain operational security is an evolving technical contest between attacker and defender. Members of the organization will need assistance in identifying and mitigating these subtle dimensions of system exposure (as well as assessing how critical they are to the mission).

Finally, there is a great emphasis on aspects of resiliency in the tasks in Table 2.1. These activities assess what is most critical to the mission and then identify means by which the mission can be acceptably carried out despite these losses. These plans must be reviewed by those higher in the hierarchy. It is not just important to evaluate whether a given unit has properly identified the risks, assessed criticality, and developed and rehearsed ways to ensure mission continuity. It is also vital to ensure that continuity plans across units are mutually consistent. If one unit's plans rely on another unit that also might be under attack, the mitigation plan is flawed. For example, a unit that depends on a data set might identify that data as mission

---

[11] See Snyder et al., 2020.

[12] Dung Vu Pham, Ali Syed, and Malka N. Halgamuge, "Universal Serial Bus Based Software Attacks and Protection Solutions," *Digital Investigation*, Vol. 7, April 2011; Nir Nissim, Ran Yahalom, and Yuval Elovici, "USB-Based Attacks," *Computers and Security*, Vol. 70, September 2017.

[13] For some examples, see Yu-ichi Hayashi, "State-of-the-Art Research on Electromagnetic Information Security," *Radio Science*, Vol. 51, No. 7, June 2016, and Mara Hvistendahl, "3D Printers Vulnerable to Spying: Design Information Can Be Pilfered from the Sounds a Printer Makes," *Science*, Vol. 352, No. 6282, April 8, 2016.

critical. In the event of loss of access to that data or loss of confidence in the integrity of that data, the unit might plan to restore access to accurate data by reaching out to another unit or organization. But that plan is weak because the other unit or organization might itself be under simultaneous attack.

## Feedback

Effective process feedback and goal setting are linked. Individuals set better goals for themselves in carrying out an overall organizational strategy if they receive effective process feedback.[14]

## Obstacles

Getting good feedback on any process management area is not easy.[15] Cybersecurity poses a number of particular challenges to effective feedback.

### Scarcity

In general, feedback on cybersecurity in the Air Force is meager.[16] Events seldom indicate clearly whether cybersecurity practices are well done or whether systems are well designed. An owner might never detect a system vulnerability, and poor operational procedures can lead to an adversary gaining undetected access to a system. An adversary might install a latent cyber weapon that lies dormant, undetected. Deliberate withholding of some information about cybersecurity-related events because of other security concerns compounds these ordinary challenges. In the absence of feedback, organizations often repeat decisions for no other reason than that is what they did before.[17] In many instances, feedback is so sparse as to leave individuals at all levels fairly ignorant of the consequences of decisions that bear on cybersecurity. Lacking much feedback on a routine basis, individuals are likely to interpret the silence to mean that the status quo is acceptable.

### Ambiguity

When feedback on cybersecurity exists, it is often ambiguous. Consider a hypothetical example of malware being discovered on a critical system. Examination of the malware using the best available forensics could lead to the conclusion that the malware was of a previously known

---

[14] Peter J. Frost and Thomas A. Mahoney, "Goal Setting and the Task Process: I. An Interactive Influence on Individual Performance," *Organizational Behavior and Human Performance*, Vol. 17, No. 2, December 1976; P. Christopher Earley, Gregory B. Northcraft, Cynthia Lee, and Terri R. Lituchy, "Impact of Process and Outcome Feedback on the Relation of Goal Setting to Task Performance," *Academy of Management Journal*, Vol. 33, No. 1, March 1990.

[15] See, for example, Scott D. Sagan, *The Limits of Safety: Organizations, Accidents, and Nuclear Weapons*, Princeton, N.J.: Princeton University Press, 1993, Ch. 5.

[16] Snyder et al., 2015, pp. 13–16.

[17] March, Sproull, and Tamuz, 1991.

type and was therefore probably not targeted to the critical system but got onto it through poor operator hygiene. Some of the feedback in this example is clear: The poor operational hygiene on this critical system is a problem and needs addressing. But what is the right lesson from the forensics? Is the risk to the mission low because the analysis is correct in assessing that the malware is benign in this environment? Or is the mission potentially at risk because the attacker had sufficiently high tradecraft to fool the best available analysts, and the malware hides code targeted at the critical system? Feedback can be difficult to discern, and different parts of the Air Force can learn different lessons from the same event.

### Ephemeral Nature

Feedback on cybersecurity is generally short lived. As technologies evolve and as new vulnerabilities and susceptibilities are discovered, feedback on what was once judged an acceptable risk can become unacceptable. An event or set of events during one period might not represent the events that might take place in a later period, after technologies evolve. Unless feedback is continuous and representative, perceptions of individuals can lag reality. Since feedback is meager, perceptions generally do lag reality, as witnessed by how often many are surprised by what can be done via cyber operations.

### Misleading Cues

Feedback on cybersecurity is sometimes misleading. When bad practices do not yield accurate feedback to individuals and organizations of the real or potential consequences, that lack of feedback is effectively positive feedback that the practices are okay. Some bad practices will be reinforced as acceptable. When individuals do the right thing, they often get little to no feedback because it is not entirely clear what constitutes exemplary behavior. An organization might very well be engaging in some bad practices, but they are not recognized as such (because of the complexity of cybersecurity) or are not detected (it is difficult to monitor everything).

### Tardiness

Feedback on cybersecurity is sometimes delayed to the point that its instructive value has eroded. The longer the time between an action and the feedback on that action, the less useful the feedback is for learning.[18] A long delay obscures the causal link between the action and the consequence.[19] Even reconstructing the causality can become challenging. If an individual makes a cybersecurity mistake and if an adversary takes advantage of it but that adversary action is not

---

[18] Daniel Kahneman, *Thinking, Fast and Slow*, New York: Farrar, Straus and Giroux, 2011, pp. 241–244.

[19] Humans often attribute causality to events that are close in time and space to a consequence, a phenomenon called the *fundamental attribution error* (see Lee Ross, "The Intuitive Psychologist and His Shortcomings: Distortions in the Attribution Process," in Leonard Berkowitz, ed., *Advances in Experimental Social Psychology*, Vol. 10, New York: Academic Press, 1977).

identified until much later, it can be difficult to reconstruct all the events and extract the appropriate lessons.

*Asymmetry*

Feedback on cybersecurity is asymmetric. Cybersecurity failures are more likely to lead to useful feedback than cybersecurity successes. A failure, when identified, is a clear indication of an issue. However, in cybersecurity, successful actions lead to nonevents and, therefore, no meaningful feedback. A very high quality plan for mission assurance in the event of a high-level cyberattack is difficult to distinguish from a mediocre one, since, absent a high-level attack, both lead to nonevents. Only during a real attack (or a very well simulated one) is it clear which is better, at which point it is too late. In the field of safety, organizations often deal with a similar challenge by posting how many consecutive days an organization has gone without an accident. This practice provides positive feedback that reflects success. While lack of accidents is an effective measure of the success of safety practices, such a simple metric for success is elusive in cybersecurity. It is difficult to define what a meaningful "cyber incident" is, much less be confident that one did not occur.

## Remedies

Since real events are insufficient for effective feedback in cybersecurity, feedback from real events needs to be augmented by artificial feedback.[20] Cognitive scientists distinguish two kinds of feedback. The first is feedback on the outcomes of an action, which is called *outcome feedback*. An example of outcome feedback is dropping a bomb at a desired point of impact and noting where it hit relative to that point. The second is feedback on causality—what actions lead to which outcomes and why, which is called *performance feedback*. An example is noting that bombs are missing their desired points of impact because of systematic errors in guidance. Research indicates that performance feedback is more useful than outcome feedback.[21] Although neither kind of feedback is straightforward in cybersecurity, performance feedback is a considerable challenge and is what we seek to augment.

Available ways to augment real events with artificial events include red teams, exercises, inspections, and elaborating real events with "near events," which, analogous to near accidents, are plausible extensions of real events that did not happen but that could have happened. Artificial events do not carry the same influence as real ones. So, to make effective performance feedback out of these artificial events, they need to be constructed with that purpose in mind.

Three attributes of an event enhance its power to change individuals beliefs. The first is the degree to which the event is a crisis, something that has a marked impact, an event or story that

---

[20] Although March, Sproull, and Tamuz, 1991, is several decades old, it is still one of the most thoughtful pieces on learning in organizations when direct feedback is sparse.

[21] Earley et al., 1990; Gary Klein, *Streetlights and Shadows: Searching for the Keys to Adaptive Decision Making*, Cambridge, Mass.: MIT Press, 2009, pp. 165–176.

is a wakeup call. A cyberattack that is decisive in a conflict would be an example of such an event. The second attribute is the degree to which the event changes how people view the world. The Stuxnet attack is an example, which shifted the paradigm of what many considered possible from cyber operations, extending the effects of cyber operations to kinetically destroying hardware. The third attribute is the degree to which the event can be memorialized in storytelling. It needs to be convincing and understandable. The simpler the event is and the more easily it can be converted into a morality tale, the more useful it is as a teaching instrument.[22]

Feedback from artificial events is best shaped to reveal performance, specifically, causal links and mission impact. It is vital that individuals understand the connection between their actions—whether the actions involve designing a system or operating a system—and the consequences to Air Force missions. Red team events, exercises, inspections, and stories of near events are best crafted for feedback when they demonstrate real mission consequences, teach something new to the target audience, and are packaged stories. The feedback and training in safety follows these principles. Consequences of poor safety practices are linked to effects in the form of specific accidents. The examples used are sometimes graphic, to the point of occasionally shocking the audience. And they are told in the form of stories to which the audience can relate. The stories are plausible and relevant to the target audience, and therefore considered valid; they become useful feedback. Similarly, cybersecurity can usefully employ red-team events, exercises, inspections, and stories of near events to enhance performance feedback. There might be an opportunity to leverage practices common throughout the Air Force, such as regular safety meetings and operational risk management processes, to serve as models for increased cyber awareness, both defense measures and resiliency to attack.

---

[22] March, Sproull, and Tamuz, 1991.

# 3. Issues for Apportioning and Coordinating the Labor

> In military affairs, as in most fields of human endeavor, opponents react to each other's moves. Although this seems obvious, it is surprisingly common for advocates of certain policies or programs to assume that the adversary does not react to our initiative.
>
> —Glenn A. Kent[1]

With the basic cybersecurity tasks now laid out in Table 2.1, we turn our attention to the issues specific to the cyber realm that must be considered to properly apportion and coordinate these tasks. The assignment of tasks to proper Air Force organizations and the determination of how these organizations should be coordinated are fundamental to the efficiency and effectiveness with which the Air Force meets its overall cybersecurity strategy. The following sections discuss a number of the important cybersecurity issues the Air Force currently faces in apportioning and coordinating these cybersecurity tasks.

## The Nature of Cybersecurity Activities

A number of activities listed in Table 2.1 (and activities done lower in the hierarchy to support these objectives) are preparatory. These are the various deliberate efforts to prepare the Air Force to be cybersecure. Some examples include reducing the exposure of systems, training personnel in sound cyber hygiene, assessing the risk of a system or mission to a specific attack type, and planning and rehearsing ways to continue a mission in the event of a cyberattack. In cyber operations, these are the activities done *before* an intrusion or attack.[2]

Other activities listed in Table 2.1 are more operational. These activities are moves and countermoves in a contest between Blue and Red forces. The nature of these activities is less deliberate and more akin to crisis management. The most prominent of these activities are those associated with detecting adversary cyber operations and responding to them. Responses include tactical intelligence, forensics on any malware, assessment of mission impact, and a response plan. Being effective—which is to say, accomplishing these tasks so that the mission is not unacceptably hampered—might require doing these tasks quite rapidly to stay inside the adversary's (Red's) observe, orient, decide, and act (OODA) loop.[3] CrowdStrike, an IT security

---

[1] Kent et al., 2008, p. 158.

[2] Matthew Monte, *Network Attacks and Exploitation: A Framework*, Indianapolis, Ind.: John Wiley & Sons, 2015, pp. 93–94, calls this part of *cyber strategy*.

[3] The OODA loop idea was coined by John Boyd. The central idea is that the player, Red or Blue, that can observe, orient, decide, and act faster than the other can gains the initiative and keeps the adversary confused. Boyd never formally published his work; for a discussion, see Lawrence Freedman, *Strategy: A History*, New York: Oxford University Press, 2013, pp. 196–201.

firm, estimates that, in 2017, an intruder needed less than two hours on average from an initial network breach to move from the first penetrated computer laterally to other computers in the network, thus establishing their presence on the network.[4] These activities of recognizing, responding to, and resolving an intrusion are truly operational: They are direct actions reacting to an adversary's actions (or potential actions) and are meant to thwart or hinder an adversary's actions. In cyber operations, these are the activities done *after* an intrusion or attack.[5]

Both sets of activities are part of an arms race between adversaries and the Air Force. Both involve dynamic moves responding to one another. In the first case, the Air Force adopts a new system, software, or procedure. An adversary then develops means to exploit these, and, in turn, the Air Force adjusts its defenses and plans for mission continuity in the face of these attacks, and so on. In the second case, an adversary penetrates a network or system; the Air Force detects the action and counters it; the adversary refines its tactics; and so on. The difference between the two is largely that the latter set operates on a very short timescale and directly interacts with an adversary, not in theory but in practice.

The first set of activities resemble activities a service typically does in its roles of organizing, training, and equipping forces to present to combatant commanders. The second set of activities resemble the warfighting role a service component command provides for a combatant commander. Issues raised for the apportioning and coordinating of tasks include (1) whether the relatively fast-paced operational activities should be carried out by the same organizations (and individuals) as the slower-paced preparatory activities and (2) whether apportioning of the tasks aligns well with existing authorities.

## Technical Aspects of Cybersecurity Activities

Just about everything in the Air Force is part of cyberspace. Nearly every decision relies on data that are stored, processed, or transmitted electronically, and nearly every mission relies on systems that use such data. But when we think about cyberspace, many of us tend to think mainly about the computers that are connected via internet protocols. These are the desktop and laptop computers, servers, routers, and other IT regularly used for the processing, storing, and transmission of data across networks. In this report, we call this segment of cyberspace *enterprise networks*.[6]

Yet, many other important systems are not part of the standard enterprise network. These systems are often not directly networked to the enterprise network, operate with diverse

---

[4] CrowdStrike, *2018 Global Threat Report: Blurring the Lines Between Statecraft and Tradecraft*, 2018.

[5] Monte, 2015, pp. 93–94, calls this part of *cyber tactics*.

[6] The term *enterprise networks*, as used in this report, encompasses approximately the same as the combined Air Force Network (AFNET) and Air Force Network–Secure (AFNET-S), as defined in AFPD 17-2 *Cyberspace Operations*, Washington, D.C.: Department of the Air Force, April 12, 2016, but we extend the term to include other internet-protocol networks.

protocols, and control real-time operations with processors that are embedded into the design of the systems. We call these systems *cyber-physical systems*.[7] They include most weapon systems, industrial control systems, the internet of things, tactical communications networks (such as Link 16), data buses on aircraft, and what DoD calls "platform IT."

Cyber-physical systems pose a number of challenges for cybersecurity beyond those enterprise networks pose.[8] Because the cybersecurity of cyber-physical systems is not cleanly separable from the functionality of the systems, cybersecurity becomes a systems engineering problem tied to the functioning of the systems themselves.[9] To manage cybersecurity of these systems, this integration requires system-specific knowledge, knowledge of how the system supports missions, and any cyber-physical–specific protocols and other technical details. Because these systems control real-time operations, typical activities, such as monitoring the data traffic for anomalies, can introduce unacceptable latency. Introducing software updates and installing software patches can be problematic if they require taking the system offline. Monitoring can also be restricted by limitations in a weapon system for weight, power, heat, and space.

The diversity of technical details and physical constraints raises the issue of what role technical expertise of systems and their role in missions should play in apportioning roles and responsibilities and how to overcome limitations on data monitoring.

## Assessing the Risk of Adversary Cyber Operations

### Entities at Risk

The risks that adversary cyber operations pose span many dimensions. One set of dimensions covers which entities are held at risk. Three distinct entities can be held at risk: data, systems, and missions. These are, of course, not independent because attacks on data can affect systems, which in turn can affect mission elements. But these three entities are distinct enough for risk assessment to merit separate discussion.

Cyber operations against data can have value to an adversary in numerous ways. The data have value in their own right when exfiltrated. Exfiltration of data can boost an adversary's

---

[7] *Cyber-physical systems* "are engineered systems that are built from, and depend upon, the seamless integration of computation and physical components" (National Science Foundation, 2019).

[8] Yosef Ashibani and Qusay H. Mahmoud, "Cyber Physical Systems Security: Analysis, Challenges and Solutions," *Computers and Security*, Vol. 68, July 2017, pp. 81–97.

[9] DoD Handbook [MIL-HDBK] 1785, *System Security Engineering Program Management Requirements*, Washington, D.C.: Department of Defense, August 1, 1995 (rescinded); Ron Ross, Michael McEvilley, and Janet Carrier Oren, *Systems Security Engineering: Considerations for a Multidisciplinary Approach in the Engineering of Trustworthy Secure Systems*, Washington, D.C.: U.S. Department of Commerce, NIST Special Publication 800-160, November 2016; Deborah Bodeau and Richard Graubart, *Cyber Resiliency Design Principles: Selective Use Throughout the Lifecycle in Conjunction With Related Disciplines*, Bedford, Mass.: MITRE Corporation, MTR170001, January 2017.

situational awareness; aid the adversary in developing countermeasures to Air Force tactics, techniques, and procedures; and accelerate an adversary's weapon system development, potentially hastening the demise of the operational utility of Air Force systems. By corrupting data, erasing data, or denying access to data, an adversary can interfere with decisionmaking and command and control. These actions can, in turn, place systems and missions at risk.

A single data set can be used by a number of different systems, individuals, and organizations to support a range of missions. Because the impacts can be so broad, assessing the risk of the exfiltration, corruption, loss, or loss of access to a set of data is multifaceted and complex. Data are often widely spread throughout networks and reside in many organizations, some outside the Air Force and outside the government. Even when a single organization nominally "owns" the data, in the sense that it alone has authority to change the data, the data generally reside on and transit through systems not under the organization's control. It might not be easy to identify all the locations that retain that data set or the nodes and links through which the data flow. A full assessment of the risk of cyber operations against data is therefore a formidable task.

Assessing the impact of cyber operations against systems and mission elements is somewhat simpler from a management point of view but by no means easy from a technical point of view. Systems generally have well-defined boundaries and interfaces. A program office often has well-defined roles and responsibilities for the management of each system, including risks to that system. Missions, and their mission elements, are likewise assigned to specific organizations that have control over and responsibility for them, including accepting risk.

However, a cyber intrusion can breach the confines of a single system and move, via system interfaces, to other systems. Risk accepted in one system can propagate to others. That propagation can affect more than one mission. Further, risk is not confined to the ware (hardware, software, and firmware); it is also a function of how operators interact with the system. Operator interaction is of concern to a program office, but how operators act is determined by specific tactics, techniques, and procedures and by the cultural habits of those actors, and those fall outside program office control.

*Timelines of Risk Assessments*

Whether the risk assessment is of data, systems, or mission elements, there is a need to assess risk across roughly two timeframes. One timeframe is that needed to support risk assessment for preparatory activities. This is the time to identify system vulnerabilities; to monitor compliance of policies, such as patching computers; to evaluate the soundness of plans for mission continuity in the event of a cyberattack; and so on. Risk assessments in this timeframe combine the dimensions of vulnerability with strategic intelligence and estimates of mission impact to yield what we call *strategic risk assessment*.[10] The timeframe for strategic risk assessment is long enough to permit deliberate decisionmaking. It is the typical timeframe for most organize, train, and equip activities.

The second timeframe is that needed to react to crises. These exigent risk assessments assess the vulnerabilities, mission impact, and tactical intelligence information in real time to respond to adversarial actions in cyberspace. We call this *tactical risk assessment*. Tactical risk assessment needs to be fast enough to remain inside the adversary's OODA loop.

Overall, risk assessment is challenged by the tremendous technical diversity of cyberspace, the vast interconnectedness of systems and missions that makes localizing risk impossible, and the need to assess risk in both deliberate and crisis contexts.

## Funding Cybersecurity Activities

Aside from the clear importance of funding levels for any activity, how funding is structured also strongly affects how cybersecurity can be managed. Structuring of funding can also enhance or impede cybersecurity. Because nearly everything is connected in some way to everything else, cybersecurity issues are not nicely partitioned into the same programmatic bins as program elements in the budget. When a desired activity for cybersecurity conveniently falls into a single program element, programming, budgeting, and executing that activity is greatly simplified. More often, a cybersecurity activity will touch many systems and mission elements, generally across many operational units, and therefore span more than one program element. The misalignment of cybersecurity activities with program elements greatly complicates properly funding cybersecurity and properly monitoring the execution of funds for cybersecurity.

These issues form the fabric of challenges for managing cybersecurity and for apportioning and coordinating cybersecurity activities across the Air Force. In the next chapter, we attempt to partially address these issues.

---

[10] Note that our use of the terms *strategic risk* and *tactical risk* differ from how they are used in the risk management framework. The risk management framework uses the term *tactical risk* to refer to risk to information systems and the term *strategic risk* to risk to an organization (National Institute of Standards and Technology [NIST], *Guide for Applying the Risk Management Framework to Federal Information Systems: A Security Life Cycle Approach*, Washington, D.C.: U.S. Department of Commerce, NIST Special Publication 800-37, rev. 1, February 2010). Our usage of the terms *tactical* and *strategic* in this context conforms to their usage in the intelligence community.

# 4. Discussion of Apportioning and Coordinating the Labor

> Because all individuals in a firm are self interested, simply delegating decision rights to them and dictating the objective function each is to maximize is not sufficient to accomplish the objective. A control system that ties the individual's interest more closely to that of the organization is required.
>
> — Michael C. Jensen and William H. Meckling[1]

> Strategy is visible as coordinated action *imposed* on a system. When I say strategy is "imposed," I mean just that. It is an exercise in centralized power, used to overcome the natural workings of a system. This coordination is unnatural in the sense that it would not occur without the hand of strategy.
>
> — Richard P. Rumelt[2]

Given the strategies and tasks and the specific difficulties these pose for cybersecurity, there are several decisions bearing on roles and responsibilities that present significant issues for the Air Force. We treat four such acute decisions in this chapter. These are by no means the only problematic areas for assigning roles and responsibilities for cybersecurity in the Air Force, but they are arguably among the largest cross-cutting issues the Air Force faces:

- How should the strategic guidance for cybersecurity be expressed in policy?
- How should the roles and responsibilities for cybersecurity risk assessment be managed in the Air Force?
- Should the provision of IT network services and the cybersecurity of the networks be managed together or separately?
- How should preparatory and operational cybersecurity activities be apportioned?

## Strategic Guidance for Cybersecurity

### Findings

The proposed strategy for cybersecurity is to limit the effects of an adversary's cyberspace operations on missions. To be successful, the adversary needs to gain access to a relevant system, know enough about it and have the capabilities to affect that system in a way that has a negative impact on a mission. A central observation about cybersecurity is that there is no technical solution to the problem, and there is no single solution.[3] Cybersecurity requires an integrated

---

[1] Michael C. Jensen and William H. Meckling, "Specific and General Knowledge, and Organizational Structure," in Lars Werin and Hans Wijkander, eds., *Contract Economics*, Oxford, U.K.: Blackwell, 1992, p. 267.

[2] Rumelt, 2011, p. 92. Italics in the original.

[3] See, for example, James Gosler and Lewis Von Thaer, *Resilient Military Systems and the Advanced Cyber Threat*, Washington, D.C.: U.S. Department of Defense, January 2013.

effort across all individuals and organizations, touching virtually all Air Force entities. The starting point, as emphasized in the last chapter, is a clear, succinct objective and strategy statement to direct and coordinate all these efforts in a way that covers all necessary actions.

The policy that comes closest to issuing cybersecurity objectives and a strategy for the entire Air Force is AFPD 17-1, 2016. From the perspective advocated in this report, it has several shortcomings.

Overall, the spirit of the document falls short of giving the clear guidance for an objective for cybersecurity and a strategy for carrying it out along the lines that we stated in Chapter 2. The lack of clarity arises from a number of interrelated characteristics of the policy.

## Objective and Strategy

The objective and strategy are not clearly stated. In concert with the rest of the DoD, AFPD 17-1 defines cybersecurity as the

> [p]revention of damage to, protection of, and restoration of computers, electronic communications systems, electronic communications services, wire communication, and electronic communication, including information contained therein, to ensure its availability, integrity, authentication, confidentiality, and nonrepudiation.[4]

In the policy, this definition serves as a proxy for an objective or strategy. However, it is not framed in a way that states to how to perform comprehensive cybersecurity, which is to say that it is not a strategy that can be broken down into comprehensive tasks, activities, or means by which it can be carried out that would effectively thwart an adversary. A breakout of leading activities, akin to that listed in Table 2.1, motivated by the strategy presented in AFPD 17-1 would be incomplete. For example, the directive does not include elements of strategy that drive cyber resiliency measures. And since the list is incomplete, the assignment of roles and responsibilities derived from it is incomplete.

The consequence is that policy throughout the Air Force is nearly bereft of any mention of the roles and responsibilities in operational organizations and functional communities for cyber resiliency activities. To determine the extent to which Air Force–level policy documents mention cybersecurity and/or cyberspace, we analyzed the following series of Air Force Instruction (AFI) documents:[5]

- Acquisition (63 series)
- Logistics
  - Logistics (20 series)
  - Maintenance (21 series)
  - Materiel Management (23 series)

---

[4] AFPD 17-1, 2016, p. 12. See also CNSSI 4009, 2015; DoDI 8500.01, p. 55.

[5] All these are available from the Air Force e-Publishing website, undated.

- Transportation (24 series)
- Logistics Staff (25 series)
- Security (31 series)
- Civil Engineering (32 series)

- Operations

  - Operations (10 series)
  - Flying Operations (11 series)
  - Nuclear, Space, Missile, Command and Control (13 series)

- Medical

  - Medical Command (40 series)
  - Health Services (41 series)
  - Medical (44 series)
  - Nursing (46 series)
  - Dental (47 series)
  - Aerospace Medicine (48 series).

Out of 90 Air Force documents analyzed, only 22 from the following series mention cybersecurity and/or cyberspace at all:

- Acquisition (63 series)
- Maintenance (21 series)
- Security (31 series)
- Operations (10 series)
- Nuclear, Space, Missile, Command and Control (13 series)
- Health Services (41 series).

No mention is made of cybersecurity and/or cyberspace at all in the following series:

- Logistics (20 series)
- Materiel Management (23 series)
- Transportation (24 series)
- Logistics Staff (25 series)
- Civil Engineering (32 series)
- Flying Operations (11 series)
- Medical Command (40 series)
- Medical (44 series)
- Nursing (46 series)
- Dental (47 series)
- Aerospace Medicine (48 series).

The 23 that do mention cybersecurity and/or cyberspace provide very little real guidance, with very little mention of the need to plan and exercise the ability to continue to operate in the face of cyberattack.

Alarmingly few Air Force organizations have explicit policy directives for developing plans for continuing operations in the event of cyberattack. They also lack guidance for how to assess the impacts of various attacks on the organizations' systems and missions, what form plans should take, how to exercise these plans, and how to evaluate the effectiveness of these plans and any residual risks. Neither does any high-level policy direct organizations to understand the operational consequences of the exfiltration of information. Despite the ubiquitous reach of cyber into every organization's missions, there is no commensurate emphasis on cybersecurity at all levels of policy, down to technical orders and tactics, techniques, and procedures.

### Blending of Cybersecurity and Provision of Services

AFPD 17-1 blends policy direction for cybersecurity with the provision of enterprise network services. Because SAF/CIO A6 has policy oversight and responsibility for the provisioning of enterprise network services, this intermingling of provision and security in policy implies a disproportionate role of the SAF/CIO A6 in cybersecurity and underemphasizes the roles of everyone else. The directive states that "responsibilities for cyberspace and IT" and, by implication, cybersecurity "are overseen by SAF/CIO A6."[6] That places cybersecurity as largely a SAF/CIO A6 problem, not one that cuts across all Air Force organizations embracing operations. This assignment leads to an inherently disproportionate emphasis on the cybersecurity of enterprise networks (and the data they store, process, and transmit) over that of cyber-physical systems. And the policy declares that it applies only to "individuals or organizations authorized by an appropriate government official to manage any portion of the AF Information Network."[7] AFPD 17-1, therefore, reinforces the notion that cybersecurity is a "mission" performed by a specialized subset of those in the Air Force to secure enterprise network systems.

Our interactions with airmen, civilians, and contractors in combat support and operational units suggest that this emphasis has led many individuals see cybersecurity as a "mission" assigned to specialized organizations or individuals. Personnel perceive their role as limited to certain conduct on desktop computers in the enterprise networks. For example, many with whom we spoke in logistics did not fully perceive maintenance, test equipment, and the weapon system itself as part of their cybersecurity training. That training was limited to the office environment, not the flight line, and cybersecurity was often seen as the responsibility of someone else, not as a shared responsibility.

### Overemphasis on Cyber Defensive Measures

The overwhelming emphasis in the policy is on cyber defensive measures over cyber resiliency measures. Since defensive measures cannot be fully effective, missions must be

---

[6] AFPD 17-1, 2016, p. 3.

[7] AFPD 17-1, 2016, p. 2.

resilient for adequate cybersecurity. Other than the resiliency of information and information systems, the mention of cyber resiliency in AFPD 17-1 is restricted to one sentence that instructs all headquarters Air Force functionals, major commands, direct reporting units, and field operating agencies to "[d]evelop and exercise contingency plans for mission assurance when operating under conditions of diminished or denied [national security system], mission critical IT and data availability."[8] The policy underemphasizes the central importance of resiliency efforts and downplays the critical role that most organizations have in executing such activities as those listed in Table 2.1.

## Absence of Thresholds

AFPD 17-1, in keeping with this definition of cybersecurity, does not mention the need to define any thresholds for prioritizing criticality of data to guard against exfiltration or an acceptable level of mission degradation as the result of a cyberattack. The sensitivity of data to exfiltration is handled via the security classification process. That process defines levels of sensitivity for data and technologies for programs and for operations. Given the great recent advances in data analytics (including data mining and artificial intelligence), that process does not adequately evaluate the sensitivity of large data sets, such as those for combat support, that, when compiled, might give an adversary critical situational awareness of Air Force activities. AFPD 17-1 also does not direct such an assessment but does direct the Air Force to, "as necessary, determine tradeoffs among mission effectiveness, cybersecurity, efficiency, survivability, resiliency, and IT interoperability."[9] That is the only implicit direction to determine thresholds for risk acceptance from cyberattacks.

In summary, AFPD 17-1 (1) lacks a clear, succinct statement of an Air Force strategy for cybersecurity that describes and assigns a complete set of roles and responsibilities, (2) does not balance cyber defensive measures and cyber resiliency measures, (3) implicitly emphasizes enterprise networks over cyber-physical systems, and (4) underemphasizes the importance of understanding thresholds. To manage operational risk, organizations need to assess the consequences to operations of varying levels of data exfiltration and cyberattack. Following the management control loop in Figure 2.1, we find that these shortcomings in high-level policy lead to

- policies in the Air Force being impoverished in instructions for roles and responsibilities for cybersecurity outside of communications units, A6 staffs, intelligence units, and other organizations with specific cyber "missions"
- diminished situational awareness (feedback) because of a lack of clear understanding of goals and roles and responsibilities
- impairment of the ability to prioritize cybersecurity risk and investments of resources

---

[8] AFPD 17-1, 2016, p. 7.

[9] AFPD 17-1, 2016, Sec. 2.5.

- gaps in actions
- lack of coordinated effort.

## Recommendations

Our central recommendation is that AFPD 17-1, or its equivalent, be shaped explicitly to be the high-level cybersecurity strategic direction in a strategies-to-tasks framework. This document should clearly set out the objective and a strategy statement for cybersecurity. It should more comprehensively break down the first level of activities that need to be done across the Air Force and assign those to the appropriate leads (akin to Table 2.1). In doing so, the directive should balance cyber defensive measures and cyber resiliency measures and balance the security of enterprise networks and cyber-physical systems. And it should clearly indicate that all individuals and organizations play a role in cybersecurity and that failure to perform that role effectively could be decisive.

If the policy were issued directly by the Secretary of the Air Force,[10] it would further emphasize that cybersecurity is an Air Force–wide activity and not a mission solely under the responsibility of the SAF/CIO A6. The policy should, in turn, be directed to all members of the Air Force, not restricted to "individuals or organizations authorized by an appropriate government official to manage any portion of the AF Information Network."[11]

These recommendations would help to clarify cybersecurity strategy and derived tasks, reveal gaps and overlaps in cybersecurity activities, and improve feedback by clarifying what needs to be done and who should do it.

In the next sections, we discuss a few specific areas in which assigning roles and responsibilities present particular challenges.

# Assessing Risk

## The Problem

### Management Considerations

Assessing any risk is a difficult endeavor at an execution level. Assessing risk for cybersecurity at the management level is compounded by overlapping authorities. Leaving cybersecurity aside for the moment, the partitioning of responsibilities for managing risk are clear. The program office (acquisition community) is responsible for risk inside the design-specification-requirement envelope of a system. Risks outside the design-specification-

---

[10] Under the authority of U.S. Code (U.S.C), Title 10, Armed Forces, Subtitle D, Air Force, Part I, Organization, Chapter 903, Department of the the Air Force, Section 9013, Secretary of the Air Force.

[11] AFPD 17-1, 2016, p. 2.

requirement envelope of a system are the responsibility of the operator (operational community) of that system.[12]

This clarity is muddled for cybersecurity risk assessment with the introduction, by statutory and regulatory direction,[13] of the chief information officer (CIO) and authorizing officials, who are appointed by and report to the CIO, for cybersecurity risk acceptance. The authorizing official is "responsible for accepting a level of risk for a system balanced with mission requirements" using the risk management framework.[14] Therefore, for assessing and accepting cybersecurity risk, there is a separate process that is not aligned with other risk acceptance decisions.

## Technical Considerations

As discussed in Chapter 3, the substantial technical differences between enterprise networks and cyber-physical systems require different skills to assess risk. Further, given the variety of technologies and system designs among cyber-physical systems, the technical skills needed for risk assessment at the system level might generally need to be specific to each cyber-physical system.

A second technical consideration is that, because of networking, technical risk for cybersecurity is not as easily partitioned into organizational boundaries as other risks. Take, for example, the discovery of a fatigue crack in a structural element of an aircraft. The program office might assess that structural integrity issues pose a risk to the fleet. In response, the program office might issue a time compliance technical order limiting certain aircraft in the fleet to a restricted flight envelope until inspections are carried out to confirm the structural integrity

---

[12] AFI 63-101/20-101, *Integrated Life Cycle Management*, Washington, D.C.: Department of the Air Force, May 9, 2017, Sec. 4.6.5.3; AFI 91-202, *The US Air Force Mishap Prevention Program*, Washington, D.C.: Department of the Air Force, June 24, 2015, Change 1, February 15, 2017, Sec. 11.1.6.1.

[13] The relevant legislation includes the Clinger-Cohen Act of 1996 (Pub. L. 104-106, National Defense Authorization Act for Fiscal Year 1996 (Divisions D and E), Section 5125, Clinger-Cohen Act of 1996); Pub. L. 107-347, *Federal Information Security Management Act of 2002*, Title III of the *E-Government Act of 2002*, December 17, 2002; U.S. Code, Title 10, Armed Forces, Subtitle A, General Military Law, Part I, Organizational and General Military Powers, Chapter 4, Office of the Secretary of Defense, Section 131, Office of the Secretary of Defense; U.S.C., Title 10, Armed Forces, Subtitle A, General Military Law, Part I, Organizational and General Military Powers, Chapter 4, Office of the Secretary of Defense, Section 142, Chief Information Officer; U.S. Code, Title 10, Armed Forces, Subtitle A, General Military Law, Part IV, Service, Supply and Procurement, Chapter 131, Planning and Coordination, Section 2223, Information Technology: Additional Responsibilities of Chief Information Officers; U.S. Code, Title 10, Armed Forces, Subtitle D, Air Force, Part I, Organization, Chapter 903, Department of the the Air Force, Section 9014, Office of the Secretary of the Air Force; U.S. Code, Title 40, Public Buildings, Property, and Works, Subtitle III, Information Technology Management, Chapter 113, Responsibility for Acquisitions of Information Technology, Subchapter II, Executive Agencies, Section 11315, Agency Chief Information Officer; and DoDI 8500.01, 2014.

[14] AFI 17-101, *Risk Management Framework (RMF) for Air Force Information Technology*, Washington, D.C.: Department of the Air Force, February 2, 2017, Sec. 2.6; see also NIST, 2010; DoDI 8510.01, *Risk Management Framework (RMF) for DoD Information Technology (IT)*, Department of Defense, March 12, 2014, Change 2, July 28, 2017.

of the aircraft. Such an assessment is one of system risk within the design-specification-requirement envelope of a system and is the prerogative of the program office. The operator of the aircraft has the right to violate these stipulations if they deem the operational consequences to outweigh the system risks. An example might be an aircraft that is deployed and on an operational mission in which it is necessary to exceed the restricted flight envelope to avoid being shot down. The mission commander can accept that risk outside design-specification-requirement envelope of a system, and the consequences are confined to that command. Cyberrisk differs. In an equivalent circumstance, because of the interconnectedness of systems, the risk the operational commander accepts may very well extend outside his or her purview.

### Strategic and Tactical Risk Assessment

As also mentioned in Chapter 3, risk needs to be assessed over two contrasting timescales. One is tactical risk assessment to support decisions after an adversary's cyber operations. The timescale for this must be quick enough to stay inside an adversary's OODA loop. The other is strategic risk assessment to support deliberate decisions before an adversary's cyber operations. This timescale is generally much longer. *The risk management framework and the authorizing official are implicitly set up to assess strategic risk.*

### *Recommendations for the Role of Authorizing Officials*

### Strategic Risk

The statutory and regulatory strictures on cyber security risk acceptance along with the technical constraints prevent a clean division of roles and responsibilities. We, nevertheless, offer some recommendations for how to better assign roles and responsibilities for cybersecurity risk assessment, with a focus on the role of authorizing officials.

To partially redress the conflicts in authorities among the program offices (acquisition community), the operational community (lead major commands and combatant commands), and the authorizing official (acting on behalf of the CIO), we propose a realignment of the authorizing officials' roles for weapon systems. The cybersecurity of any weapon system, indeed any system, arises from a combination of system properties and how the system is used. The relevant properties of a system for cybersecurity are a function of the full life cycle of the system, from design to disposal. Design is critical because such attributes as the architecture of the system are locked in at that phase, and the architecture can either bolster security or limit the ability to secure the system.

Much attention is given in cybersecurity to finding vulnerabilities in systems, seeking technical fixes to the vulnerabilities (e.g., security controls), applying the proposed fixes, and monitoring the compliance with them.[15] However, how humans interact and use a system can be

---

[15] NIST, *Security and Privacy Controls for Federal Information Systems and Organizations*, Washington, D.C.: U.S. Department of Commerce, NIST Special Publication 800-53, rev. 4, April 2013; CNSSI 1253, *Security*

as important as the system attributes. Even a well-designed system can be exploited because of poor operational procedures, an insider threat, or penetration of the supply chain. As emphasized throughout this report, cybersecurity is an enterprisewide responsibility. Solutions to a vulnerability might be available either by changing the system or changing how the system is used. For legacy systems, nonmateriel solutions are generally cheaper than materiel solutions.

As the risk acceptance process is implemented through the risk management framework in the Air Force, undue emphasis is placed on systems. System vulnerabilities are emphasized over operational vulnerabilities. How a cyber incident affects systems is emphasized over how it affects a mission. And materiel mitigations directed to program offices are emphasized over nonmateriel mitigations directed at operators.

We propose a restructuring of the risk assessment and acceptance process that places system and mission attributes on an equal footing. The idea is depicted in Figure 4.1. At the center of the proposal is that system and operational (mission) risk be assessed independently by equally resourced entities that are mutual peers. The system risk assessment would be done as it is currently done, by what the risk management framework refers to as *security control assessors*. We advocate changing the name of this position to *system risk assessor* (SRA). That change will emphasize that the role is to assess risk to the system, not the very restrictive action of recommending and evaluating the implementation of discrete security controls. For weapon systems, this person would represent the concerns of the program office. The SRA would identify vulnerabilities at the system level, assess the risks these pose to the functioning of the system, and propose solutions that are often materiel in nature. The SRA would assess risk *inside* the design-specification-requirement envelope of a system.

Each system would be uniquely assigned to an SRA for risk assessment. An assessment of the risk of each interface between any two systems would be assessed by the two relevant SRAs (or a single SRA if both systems are assigned to one SRA). This process would supplement the process of assessing the risk of connecting a system to AFNET; it would assess the risk of connecting any two systems (e.g., connecting test equipment with an aircraft).

Mirroring the SRA would be an operational risk assessor (ORA), a newly created position on par with the SRA. The ORA would identify critical mission elements; assess the risks system failures pose to the mission elements; and propose solutions in the form of changes in tactics, techniques, and procedures. The ORA would take a mission-perspective on cybersecurity, represent the interests of the lead major commands, and be appointed by them. The boundaries of the ORA's jurisdiction would be mission boundaries. The ORA would assess risk *outside* the design-specification-requirement envelope of systems.

---

*Categorization and Control Selection for National Security Systems*, Committee on National Security Systems, March 27, 2014.

**Figure 4.1. Proposed Structure for Authorizing Officials for Weapon Systems**

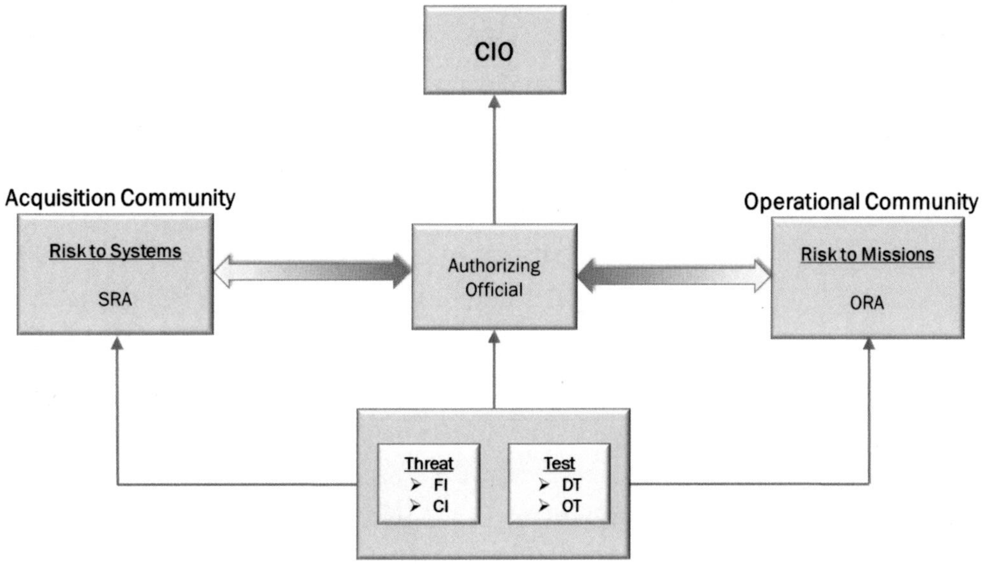

NOTE: The arrows represent dominant information flow. CI = counterintelligence; DT = developmental test; FI = foreign intelligence; and OT = operational test.

The authorizing official would take the system and operational risk assessments the appropriate SRAs and ORAs provide and decide on what risks to accept. The boundaries of jurisdiction of authorizing officials would be mission boundaries. All parties, as shown in Figure 4.1, would get all relevant intelligence and test information pertinent to their purview. Having the vantage point of seeing both risks and potential mitigations, the authorizing official would be well placed to judge where resources should be applied to get the most operational benefit with the least resource investment, whether solutions fall on the materiel or nonmateriel side.

To facilitate cybersecurity actions, the authorizing official would be given a budget to allocate for cybersecurity. This budget could be used to identify issues or to resolve issues already identified, at the discretion of the authorizing official. Giving the authorizing official a budget would have several positive effects. Currently, an authorizing official might accept risk in an area and recommend taking certain actions to resolve identified or emerging cybersecurity issues. But absent a budget to address such issues, they often remain unaddressed. It would incentivize authorizing officials to prioritize remediations that may be beyond the means or priorities of a single program or operational function but that have a broader impact across their assigned mission area. It would also incentivize the program offices and operational units to identify cybersecurity issues as they compete for funds from the authorizing official. And it would fence resources for resolving cybersecurity issues and improve visibility of the use of those funds.

To carry out these extended duties, the authorizing officials would need to be dedicated to this one job and be equipped with a staff. The staff would need to have the ability to manage and execute a program element, adjudicate among the SRAs and ORAs, and receive and process threat and test information relevant to their portfolio of risk acceptance decisions.

## Tactical Risk

When confronting tasks that require quick response (e.g., those related to tactical risk) and tasks that require longer deliberation (e.g., those related to strategic risk), assigning these to the same organization is sometimes problematic.[16] The type of organizational structure that can more efficiently manage quick-response tasks differs from one that can better manage longer term, deliberative tasks. Short-term tasks require organizations to be more responsive. In general, an organization is more responsive when tasks are decentralized,[17] especially so when decentralized subunits are coordinated through horizontal communication mechanisms.[18] Highly specialized differentiated subunits can more quickly adapt to a changing environment.[19] Fewer levels of hierarchy (which usually exist in these decentralized organizations) mean that the chain of command is shorter, leading to fewer bottlenecks in the process to achieve a responsive outcome.[20] Longer-term, deliberative tasks do not require this level of flexibility and agility, and can be more economically organized using a more hierarchical, centralized structure.[21]

When tasks of such different timescales are assigned to the same organization, the organization faces competing demands.[22] The possibility emerges that either the shorter-term

---

[16] See, for example, Gregory A Bigley and Karlene H. Roberts, "The Incident Command System: High-Reliability Organizing for Complex and Volatile Task Environments," *Academy of Management Journal*, Vol. 44, No. 6, December 2001.

[17] Mintzberg, 1979, p. 270; Massimo G. Colombo and Marco Delmastro, "Delegation of Authority in Business Organizations: An Empirical Test," *Journal of Industrial Economics*, Vol. 52, No. 1, March 2004; Jennifer C. Coats and Frederick W. Rankin, "The Delegation of Decision Rights: An Experimental Investigation," in Marc J. Epstein and Mary A. Malina, eds., *Advances in Management Accounting*, Vol. 27, Bingley, U.K.: Emerald Group Publishing, 2016.

[18] Mintzberg, 1979, p. 270. Also see Robert C. Ford and W. Alan Randolph, "Cross-Functional Structures: A Review and Integration of Matrix Organization and Project Management," *Journal of Management,* Vol. 18, No. 2, June 1992, for a review of extensive literature supporting this.

[19] Ricardo Alonso, Wouter Dessein, and Niko Matouschek, "Organizing to Adapt and Compete," *American Economic Journal: Microeconomics*, Vol. 7, No. 2, May 2015.

[20] Oliver E. Williamson, "Hierarchical Control and Optimum Firm Size," *Journal of Political Economy*, Vol. 75, No. 2, April 1967; Guillermo A. Calvo and Stanislaw Wellisz, "Supervision, Loss of Control, and the Optimal Size of the Firm," *Journal of Political Economy*, Vol. 86, No. 5, October 1978; Raghuram G. Rajan and Julie Wulf, "The Flattening Firm: Evidence from Panel Data on the Changing Nature of Corporate Hierarchies," *Review of Economics and Statistics*, Vol. 88, No. 4, November 2006.

[21] Decentralization may require some redundancy of positions and additional costs to coordinate (e.g., move information) among differentiated subunits. See, for instance, Jay R. Galbraith, *Designing Complex Organizations*, Reading, Mass.: Addison-Wesley, 1973; Jensen and Meckling, 1992; and Thomas W. Malone, *The Future of Work: How the New Order of Business Will Shape Your Organization, Your Management Style and Your Life*, Boston, Mass.: Harvard Business School Press, 2004.

[22] See Medhanie Gaim, Nils Wåhlin, Miguel Pina e Cunha, and Stewart Clegg, "Analyzing Competing Demands in Organizations: A Systematic Comparison," *Journal of Organization Design*, Vol. 7, No. 1, December 2018, and references therein.

activities will get priority over the longer-term ones, or the shorter-term activities will not get done in time because resources are distracted by longer-term tasks. This competition could be a source of friction for executing these different tasks.

Yet divorcing tactical and strategic risk assessment for a given system or mission creates a seam in oversight and makes inconsistent assessments likely. As of the writing of this report in 2018, authorizing officials perform cyber risk acceptance decisions on top of other duties. Not only does tactical risk assessment require quick response, but during a crisis, the number of simultaneous incidents to address could be quite high. The current authorizing official structure is not conducive to the quick response needed for tactical risk assessment and decisionmaking and does not scale well to a crisis.

One way to resolve some of these challenges is to assign tactical risk assessment and decisionmaking for cyber risk acceptance to the operational authorities responsible for incident response. An adjustment to policy would be needed to accommodate this change. If such a change were made, to mitigate creating an inconsistency between tactical and strategic risk assessment, policy should state that the relevant authorizing official be consulted, formalizing lateral communications between the two tasks.[23] Further, to support both tactical and strategic risk assessments, policy should mandate that all information relevant to the cybersecurity of any system be deposited in a standardized repository. This process could be modeled after the aircraft structural integrity program.[24]

Such a cybersecurity integrity program would be established for each system. It would archive all relevant threat data for that system, test information relevant to cybersecurity, any cybersecurity vulnerabilities identified in the system, and any system-related mitigations that have been implemented. This would be a permanent record for the system for cybersecurity that could be consulted during crises to facilitate decisionmaking (similar to how an emergency physician can make better decisions, and perhaps avoid mistakes, by consulting a patient's medical record).

## Provisioning Services and Performing Security

Consider now just the enterprise network side of cyberspace—excluding weapon systems, industrial control systems, the internet of things, and similar entities. All organizations are confronted by two task groupings for these systems: the provisioning of the service and the cybersecurity of the networks.

---

[23] Richard L. Daft, *Organization Theory and Design*, 9th ed., Mason, Ohio: Thomson South-Western, 2007.

[24] AFI 63-140, *Aircraft Structural Integrity Program*, Washington, D.C.: Department of the Air Force, April 7, 2014.

In the commercial sector, these two task groupings are generally separated into distinct disciplines that are often called *IT services* and *information security* (InfoSec).[25] These roles are nearly always assigned to different organizations because of fundamental differences in their activities. IT manages cyber services (operations and maintenance of computer systems, networks, and data), requirements planning, knowledge management and in-house software and systems development, computer user and network support, and software assurance. InfoSec deals with protecting and defending systems and networks, security incidents, information assurance compliance, security system development, and designing system security architectures.

IT services operate in a relatively stable environment and are less complex than InfoSec, while the InfoSec environment is more variable and more complex. Because of the inherent unpredictability of the InfoSec environment and the higher degrees of uncertainty and disorder, InfoSec personnel need more autonomy in decisionmaking. IT and InfoSec are considered two separate career tracks, and staff rarely transition from one to the other. To coordinate across disciplines, commercial industry employs strong lateral linkages between IT and InfoSec, both formal and informal, forming committees and working groups to foster relationships.

Centralized IT departments yield better organizational outcomes than those with decentralized responsibilities.[26] Centralization provides a more professional operation, efficient use of staff and equipment, multiple access to common data, assurance of data standards, and availability of specialized staff. Top management retains decision rights, and the organization has the ability to establish uniformity, which reduces complexity and enables operations at scale. However, in practice, the choice between centralization and decentralization for IT often matches the style of the overall organization.[27]

In contrast, responsiveness is crucial in the InfoSec environment, and InfoSec departments are generally more decentralized.[28] Decentralized decisionmaking increases responsiveness by providing greater user control; easier access to data; the ability to meet the needs of individual units; and access to the best local, relevant knowledge.[29] In the corporate world, InfoSec is generally viewed as a corporate governance responsibility and, thus, is a business issue, not a

---

[25] This section draws heavily on Lara Schmidt, Caolionn O'Connell, Hirokazu Miyake, Akhil R. Shah, Joshua William Baron, Geof Nieboer, Rose Jourdan, David Senty, Zev Winkelman, Louise Taggart, Susanne Sondergaard, and Neil Robinson, *Cyber Practices: What Can the U.S. Air Force Learn From the Commercial Sector?* Santa Monica, Calif.: RAND Corporation, RR-847-AF, 2015.

[26] James S. Denford, Gregory S. Dawson, and Kevin C. Desouza, "An Argument for Centralization of IT Governance in the Public Sector," presented at the 48th Hawaii International Conference on System Sciences, Kauai, Hawaii, 2015.

[27] Allen E. Brown and Gerald G. Grant, "Framing the Frameworks: A Review of IT Governance Research," *Communications of the Association for Information Systems*, Vol. 15, No. 38, May 2005; Roger Alan Pick, "Shepherd or Servant: Centralization and Decentralization in Information Technology Governance," *International Journal of Management & Information Systems*, Vol. 19, No. 2, 2nd Qtr. 2015.

[28] Schmidt et al., 2015.

[29] Brown and Grant, 2005; Pick, 2015.

technical issue.[30] In many companies, the InfoSec function is tightly integrated into the overall corporate risk-management process, and decisions about security posture and investments are made from a business risk perspective, not an IT perspective.

In the Air Force, these functions, which are separate IT and InfoSec departments in the commercial sector, are intertwined. Many organizations throughout the Air Force have responsibilities for both provisioning and securing enterprise networks. Personnel move back and forth between providing network services and security tasks, sometimes within the same workday, and the corresponding career fields are not clearly distinguished.

## Preparatory and Operational Cybersecurity Activities

An underlying theme runs through the activities in Table 2.1 and the discussion in this chapter, that cybersecurity activities cluster into two groups. One group consists of activities that must be done rapidly, require some detailed knowledge (of mission, tactics, systems, etc.), and are often complex. The other group consists of activities that can be done more deliberately, require less detailed knowledge, and are less complex.

The starkest example is the separation of activities that are preparatory—done *before* an intrusion or attack—and those that are operational—done *after* an intrusion or attack and are performed to respond to those events. To be successful, the operational activities must act quickly to stay within an active adversary's OODA loop. Those performing operational activities must have a breadth and depth of knowledge to outwit the adversary and in a fairly complex environment.

As we argued when discussing risk assessment and how the corporate sector typically manages its enterprise networks, these challenges are most often met by assigning preparatory and operational duties to different organizations. Separation is useful to avoid conflicting demands in a single organization. Some of these conflicting demands are between short-term (e.g., incident response) and long-term (e.g., installing a network upgrade) objectives. Conflicts can also arise between dueling short-term demands. For example, within the same organization, applying time-sensitive prophylactic patches can compete with responding to help-desk tickets.

Separation is also useful because organizations performing fast, complex operations tend to be decentralized. They push decisions to lower levels in the organization to decrease decision time, to increase flexibility, and to place decisions closer to the locus of relevant information. Coordination of effort is achieved through strong horizontal coordination mechanisms. Organizations performing more-deliberate but less-complex tasks tend to centralize. Centralization in its extreme form concentrates control within the organization of the collection of information, the processing of that information, making decisions, authorizing actions, and

---

[30] Basie von Solms and Rossouw von Solms, "The 10 Deadly Sins of Information Security Management," *Computers and Security*, Vol. 23, No. 5 July 2004.

executing the actions. The more deliberate and simpler the circumstances, the more these activities can be centralized in an organization.[31]

Preparatory and operational activities can be separated without placing them in two separate organizations. A single organization can have mixed structures to accommodate the differing needs of each subdivision.[32]

In contrast with the commercial sector, preparatory and operational activities are not well separated in the Air Force. Strategic and tactical cyberthreat analyses are fairly well separated in the intelligence community. But for most areas outside intelligence support, the separation is less distinct. For risk assessment and acceptance, no explicit distinction is made between the strategic and tactical settings. For incident response, duties for the enterprise networks are assigned to units in the 16th Air Force. However, for incident response for cyber-physical systems, authorities and roles and responsibilities are evolving and less clear. In the Air Force, A6 staffs and communications squadrons are responsible for both of the functions that are called IT services and InfoSec in the commercial world.

There is no right or wrong way to structure an organization. Each way of assigning responsibilities comes with advantages and disadvantages. For example, separating strategic and tactical risk assessment into separate organizations, with strategic risk assessment done by authorizing officials and with tactical risk assessment embedded in an organization handling incident response, would allow each organization to be optimized for the demands of its task environment. Strategic risk could be better standardized and better coordinated across the enterprise. Tactical risk could be more responsive and could empower those with exquisite knowledge to find clever solutions to mitigate risk. However, there are drawbacks. Because of the interconnectedness of cyberspace, decisions regarding risk at a system level can have effects well beyond that one system. Decentralized decisionmaking can lead to enterprise regrets.

For the blending of enterprise network provisioning and operational activities in A6 staffs and communications squadrons, the benefits are less clear. Coordination of effort has some advantages, but, as shown in the commercial sector, the tasks are sufficiently different to merit separation of both organizations and career fields. Well-intentioned statutory and regulatory constraints impede this separation, and many of these responsibilities are blended in the duties assigned to the agency CIOs.

These characteristics of activities and their relevance to organizational design need to be considered more deliberately. When rewriting high-level policy, such as AFPD 17-1, activities that require quick decisions using detailed knowledge in a complex environment should be distinguished from those that do not. Exactly how these activities should be grouped will depend on the details of each case and how much of what kinds of enterprise risk the Air Force wishes to take.

---

[31] Mintzberg, 1979, pp. 187–188.

[32] Burton, Obel, and Håkonsson, 2015.

# 5. Improving the Cyber Culture

> Real advanced technology—on-the-edge sophisticated technology—issues not from knowledge but from something I will call *deep craft*. Deep craft is more than knowledge. It is a set of knowings. Knowing what is likely to work and what not to work. Knowing what methods to use, what principles are likely to succeed, what parameter values to use in a given technique. Knowing whom to talk to down the corridor to get things working, how to fix things that go wrong, what to ignore, what theories to look to. This sort of craft-knowing takes science for granted and mere knowledge for granted. And it derives collectively from a shared culture of beliefs, an unspoken culture of common experience.
>
> — W. Brian Arthur.[1]

Members of an organization occasionally need to solve problems that are not specifically addressed by its written rules. Sometimes problems they encounter are technical and beyond the ability of those writing rules higher in the hierarchy to solve. Other times, the problems that they encounter are dynamic or situational, posing challenges that rule writers cannot keep up with. The latter can happen in normal circumstances but becomes acute during crises. The cyber realm contains many instances of both cases, having both highly technical and rapidly evolving facets. It requires deep craft. It is in these circumstances that the organization's culture guides its members.

Organizational culture can be defined as

> the pattern of basic assumptions that a given group has invented, discovered, or developed in learning to cope with its problems of external adaptation and internal integration, and that have worked well enough to be considered valid, and, therefore, to be taught to new members as the correct way to perceive, think, and feel in relation to those problems.[2]

By this definition, the cyber culture in the Air Force is in its early stages of development. Aside from those whose direct job responsibilities focus on cybersecurity, our interactions with airmen, civilians, and contractors indicate that they share few common assumptions about cybersecurity and, occasionally, have conflicting assumptions. The cyberthreat is also relatively new, and the service has yet to fight a high-end battle in cyberspace, so the organization has yet to fully develop coping strategies. The coping strategies developed so far have not been put to the test in such a way that convinces members of the Air Force that the strategies are sufficiently valid to adapt to the cyberthreat or to internally coordinate efforts to do so and are therefore not

---

[1] W. Brian Arthur, *The Nature of Technology: What It Is and How It Evolves*, New York: Free Press, 2009, pp. 159–160; italics in the original.

[2] Edgar H. Schein, "Coming to a New Awareness of Organizational Culture," *Sloan Management Review*, Vol. 25, No. 2, Winter 1984, p. 3.

yet universally "considered valid" as the "correct way to perceive, think, and feel." What can leaders do to improve the cyber culture, both in focus and in strength?

## Defining the Culture

Leaders first need to determine what shared assumptions about cybersecurity they want all individuals in the Air Force to hold.[3] These are not limited to the shared assumptions of the cadre of workers who in some sense specialize in cybersecurity; rather, these are the shared beliefs that all individuals should hold in common (airmen, civilians, and contractors), regardless of career field or job assignment. These beliefs and associated values form the glue that binds the actors to achieve cybersecurity objectives in a complex, evolving environment. It is one of the important factors that defines how the group will behave when encountering a problem not treated in written rules and how coordinated that effort will be.

The extent to which these assumptions are shared across the Air Force, the intensity with which the beliefs are held, and the stability of these assumptions over time determine the strength of the culture. Evidence suggests that organizations with strong cultures may be more successful than those with weak cultures.[4] But the strength of a culture is only helpful to the extent that the collective assumptions that an organization's members hold are well suited to help it adapt to external conditions and achieve internal integration.[5]

The following subsections present some beliefs and assumptions that all airmen, civilians, and contractors ought to share, yet present challenges to leaders to inculcate.

### A Sense That There Is Conflict in Cyberspace Between the United States and Others That Is Ubiquitous in Time and Space

This cultural element presents challenges because it contrasts with most of the other threats that the Air Force encounters. Other threats rise when at a deployed location, under the operational command of a combatant commander, and during warfighting contingencies. Non-cyber threats fall to nearly zero when at home station; at lower alert conditions; and while performing organize, train, and equip activities.[6] But cyberthreats differ in having a less clean demarcation. The aggressiveness and number of attempted cyber operations will undoubtedly

---

[3] Throughout this chapter, the term *leader* will refer to any officer or civilian in a leadership position in the Air Force across all functional areas (e.g., logistics, intelligence, medical, life-cycle management). It is not restricted to the chain of command or to the operational or IT side of the Air Force.

[4] Daniel R. Denison and Aneil K. Mishra, "Toward a Theory of Organizational Culture and Effectiveness," *Organization Science*, Vol. 6, No. 2, March–April 1995; Larry Mallak, "Understanding and Changing Your Organization's Culture," *Industrial Management*, Vol. 43, No. 2, March–April 2001.

[5] Schein, 1984, p. 7.

[6] Per policy, operational security is not focused solely on deployments, but the culture places a higher awareness of operational security on deployments (see DoD Directive 5205.02E, *DoD Operations Security (OPSEC) Program*, Department of Defense, June 20, 2012, Change 1, May 11, 2018).

increase during wartime, but cyber intrusions for data exfiltration, intelligence preparation of the battlefield, and attack are significant at home during peacetime. That means a degree of awareness and vigilance is needed for cybersecurity that contrasts with other operational threats. Embedding a cyber subculture of persistent threat awareness and vigilance clashes with a broader culture of swings of threat awareness between peacetime and wartime operations. Members also have incomplete situational awareness of the range and nature of these cyber activities, which also contributes to the challenge of inculcating this cultural element.

### A Sense That Operations in Cyberspace Might Be Decisive in Warfare

Cyber capabilities are no longer just enabling; they are integral to nearly every aspect of Air Force activities. The United States has never been subjected to the full capabilities of a nation state attacking its systems and data through cyberspace. As of this writing, no aircraft has ever fallen out of the sky because of a cyberattack, and no base has ever had its supply chain entirely cut off because of a cyberattack. Again, many of the activities that have happened and the effects that might be possible are not widely shared, often for other security reasons. So, calibrating Air Force assumptions about what is reasonably possible is, therefore, not reinforced by direct, empirical feedback. To the contrary, the feedback that most individuals get is that nothing really bad happens and that, even when they commit bad practices (like poor cyber hygiene), there are no major consequences to the mission. This false sense of security is reinforced by the experiences most members have with IT in their private lives. It is challenging to ask them to view security with a computer one way when on duty (or at work) when they have different habits at home. The problem is compounded by the observation that different age groups view cybersecurity differently.[7] Even when good habits are learned, research indicates that people are not good at transferring good security habits learned for one device type (e.g., home computer) to another (e.g., mobile devices).[8] Without accurate feedback, other mechanisms are needed to establish sound beliefs "well enough to be considered valid" that cyber operations might be decisive.[9]

---

[7] Adéle da Veiga and Nico Martins, "Defining and Identifying Dominant Information Security Cultures and Subcultures," *Computers and Security*, Vol. 70, September 2017.

[8] Nik Thompson, Tanya Jane McGill, and Xuequn Wang, "'Security Begins at Home:' Determinants of Home Computer and Mobile Device Security Behavior," *Computers and Security*, Vol. 70, September 2017; Ron Bitton, Andrey Finkelstein, Lior Sidi, Rami Puzis, Lior Rokach, and Asaf Shabtai, "Taxonomy of Mobile Users' Security Awareness," *Computers and Security*, Vol. 73, March 2018.

[9] Schein, 1984, p. 3.

## An Understanding That All Airmen, Civilians, and Contractors Play a Role in Cybersecurity

There are cyber operators in the Air Force, and there are Air Force specialty codes centered on cybersecurity.[10] Whole organizations are dedicated to some form of cybersecurity or other cyber operations. Yet, by their actions, every actor in the Air Force can present vulnerabilities to the Air Force. And every actor in the Air Force has responsibilities to prepare and to carry out their assigned missions even in the event of loss of data, systems, or communications because of cyberattack. But the existence of organizations and individuals who have dedicated responsibilities to cybersecurity can engender a sense among others that cybersecurity responsibilities are confined to these specialists.

## A Realization That Nothing Can Be Completely Secure in Cyberspace

While it is true that nothing can be completely secure, measures to increase security and mission resiliency are not futile. They increase the resources that an adversary must apply and decrease the likelihood that the attacker will significantly impair an Air Force mission. Like other risks, the risks from threats through cyberspace cannot be brought to zero, but risks can and should be reduced. When communicating the message that nothing can be completely secure, leaders should be attentive that the message conveyed engenders vigilance, not despondency. This realization leads to a shared responsibility:

## A Sense of Responsibility to Carry on Their Mission(s) in the Face of an Attack Through Cyberspace

Some organizations are assigned specific duties, such as gathering intelligence, guarding networks, and responding to incidents, but everyone has a responsibility to carry on their mission should these efforts fail. And they should not assume that these efforts will not fail. This responsibility is not unique to cybersecurity. Base support does not have the direct responsibility for protecting a runway from missile and bomb attack, but it does have the responsibility for rapid runway repair in the event that missiles or bombs get through defenses. Likewise, a maintainer or supply manager does not have direct responsibilities to defend the computers and networks that they use. But they do have a responsibility to carry on their mission should they lose access to data or connectivity or if their data are corrupted. This realization should be deeply engrained in all through rehearsals and realistic exercises that force every individual to think through and practice executing their responsibilities in the face of a cyberattack. Diffusing an accurate sense of what might befall a mission because of a cyberattack is hampered by the sensitivities of widely revealing threat information and where the vulnerabilities of Air Force systems lie.

---

[10] For example, the officer 17D*x* and enlisted 1B4*xx* Air Force specialty codes.

## A Sense That Connecting a System to Another (or a Network) Carries Potential Risks

Every interconnection of a system to another (or a network) expands the exposure of the systems. Some of these connections are subtle. When a vendor servicing a system connects their laptop to an Air Force system that is otherwise not connected to a network, that system has, briefly, been connected to that laptop and whatever networks that laptop was connected to in the past. Some risk/benefit assessment should be done before any connections are made. This cultural element has two corollaries: (1) No two systems should be connected electronically without explicit authorization, and (2) any observed unexpected or abnormal connections should be reported. This cultural element is difficult to impute as it goes counter to two broader culture forces: that of society, in which functionality generally wins over security in market forces that drive the IT sector, and that of the Air Force, which is pushing to exploit the operational benefits of interconnectivity.

## A Sense of Obligation to Report Anomalies in Data, Nonnominal Procedures, and Potential Cyber Incidents

The cyber domain is so complex and so dynamic that no written policies will anticipate all contingencies.[11] To be adaptive and make decisions on the fly, actors at all levels need constant feedback for adequate situational awareness. Every airman, civilian, and contractor is a potential agent for reporting potential cyber incidents, including data loss, data corruption, and loss of connectivity. But some reporting also needs to extend to incidents that are not obviously cyber related, such as systemic failure of some component on a weapon system. Is the systemic failure due to "normal" failure or to an attack? The challenge is obvious—discerning what is worthy of reporting from that which is not. Calibration of a sense of what to report is critical: Underreporting leads to errors of omission; overreporting dissipates resources on unproductive activities and can desensitize individuals of real incidents.[12]

## Changing the Culture

Three themes run through the challenges for inculcating these cultural elements. First, many of the cultural beliefs and assumptions desired for cybersecurity run counter to existing cultural assumptions. Second, either a lack of feedback or feedback that runs counter to the desired cyber beliefs or assumptions impedes the ability to indelibly embed cultural assumptions "well enough to be considered valid, and, therefore, to be taught to new members as the correct way to

---

[11] Snyder et al., 2015.

[12] Don Snyder, Elizabeth Bodine-Baron, Mahyar A. Amouzegar, Kristin F. Lynch, Mary Lee, and John G. Drew, *Robust and Resilient Logistics Operations in a Degraded Information Environment*, Santa Monica, Calif.: RAND Corporation, RR-2015-AF, 2017, treats this question in depth for logistics, but most of the discussion in that report is applicable beyond the logistics field.

perceive, think, and feel."[13] Third, the countervailing need to withhold some information from individuals because of other security concerns frustrates situational awareness (e.g., not revealing sources and methods in intelligence, not revealing vulnerabilities of Air Force systems). What tools do leaders have to overcome these challenges?

In a broad review of the literature, Fernandez and Rainey identified eight actions that public-sector institutions employ when they succeed in cultural change.[14] The following subsections address each and adapt them to the present context.

## Persuade People That a Cultural Change Is Needed

To change the culture throughout an organization, each member needs to believe there is a need for the change. They need to understand that there is a problem to solve and, often, that the need for resolution is urgent enough for attention. The lack of a decisive blow through cyberspace to date and the mixed, ambiguous signals about the cyber risk have muddied this message. The classification of much of the cyber threat information and details of vulnerabilities have also hampered the effort of persuading the Air Force members that a cultural shift is needed. This need lies at the root of our recommendation that each airman, civilian, and contractor understand that operations in cyberspace might be decisive in warfare. Senior leaders and commanders need to take the lead in making this case.

## Ensure Support and Commitment of Senior Leadership and Commanders

Research indicates that most cultural change comes from the top leaders in an organization.[15] In the Air Force, the culture must be driven by the command chain, from the top down. The highest effect would come from consistent messaging from the Secretary and Chief of Staff. In the public sector, it has been found that significant changes often also have the support of career civil servants, as they hold positions longer than military officers and can, when opposed, outlast more transient managers.[16]

For implanting culture, actions are more important than words. Organization members notice what leaders do more than what they say. Perhaps the most important action for transmitting culture is what leaders pay attention to and what they regularly monitor. One company's leaders emphasize the importance of safety by starting all meetings by discussing the safety issues of the

---

[13] Schein, 1984, p. 3.

[14] The eight actions (factors) listed are paraphrased from Sergio Fernandez and Hal G. Rainey, "Managing Successful Organizational Change in the Public Sector," *Public Administration Review*, Vol. 66, No. 2, March–April 2006, to apply them directly to the cyber cultural elements in the Air Force. We have also changed the order of the actions (factors), which is arbitrary. Parts of the discussion also draw heavily on Edgar H. Schein, and Peter Schein, *Organizational Culture and Leadership*, 5th ed., Hoboken, N.J.: John Wiley & Sons, 2017, Ch. 10, adapting the content of that chapter to the context of cybersecurity in the Air Force.

[15] Schein, 1984, p. 8.

[16] Fernandez and Rainey, 2006.

day.[17] Even if the mention is brief, it highlights the importance of the topic; members of the organization prepare themselves in anticipation. Leadership attention and member preparation eventually impresses a concern for safety that becomes part of the cultural of the organization. Small, consistent actions like this across the Air Force can also impress cybersecurity on the culture.

Selectively choosing what leaders get emotional about provides an additional mechanism for reinforcing cultural norms. Many good leaders limit emotional outbursts. But when a good leader does get angry about something, that sends a strong signal of the importance of that matter. If a leader gets angry that an infraction of cybersecurity occurs even though it leads to some (perhaps short-term) operational efficiency, that emotional outburst will be noticed over policy statements and clearly indicate the priority to get the cybersecurity right. Again, these reactions must be coherent across the enterprise to be most effective.

## Present a Clear and Coherent Plan for Change

To instill a changed culture, leaders need a clear, coherent plan. This need strongly reinforces the message of Chapter 2 of this report: Leaders need to define a clear objective, a coherent strategy to achieve that objective, and specific coordinated tasks tied to that strategy that are apportioned across the Air Force. Clarity is needed to avoid confusion among members and to hold members accountable for deviating from the plan. Coherence is needed to avoid conflicting actions and to avoid gaps in security. Unclear, incoherent plans allow members of an organization to ad lib their own interpretations of objectives and strategies. A strategy-to-tasks framework provides a coordinating mechanism to develop a clear, coherent plan.

## Build Internal Support for Change and Overcome Any Resistance

Change is often resisted, both by individuals and organizations. Concerted effort is required to overcome this inertia. Two circumstances have been found to assist in pushing an organization through change.

The first circumstance is a shock to the organization, often generated out of a crisis, or what Kets de Vries and Balazs call a *focal event*.[18] A focal event can be a real crisis, such as Pearl Harbor, Sputnik, or 9/11. Clearly, waiting for such a cyber crisis is not desirable. It is preferable to create this sense of urgency out of a staged focal event. The usefulness of staged focal events reinforces the point made at the close of Chapter 2 on the utility of red-team events, exercises, inspections, and stories of "near events" to enhance performance feedback. As we argued, staged focal events are most effective when crafted to be a wakeup call, to change how members of the Air Force view cybersecurity, and to be easily memorialized in storytelling.

---

[17] Schein and Schein, 2017, p. 184.

[18] Manfred F. R. Kets de Vries and Katharina Balazs, "Transforming the Mind-Set of the Organization: A Clinical Perspective," *Administration & Society*, Vol. 30, No. 6, January 1999.

Along the same lines, members of an organization are strongly affected by how leaders respond and act during real crises. During crises or other times of abnormality, they look to the reaction of leaders and commanders for insights into the real values of the organization. Consider a systemic maintenance problem whose cause is not initially understood. Perhaps it is a weapon release that systemically fails. Under such circumstances, a "107 request" is filed to seek advice from the program office.[19] If, as part of this process, or augmenting it, leaders or commanders also examined the possibility of cyber operations as a cause, it would show that leaders consider cyber threats a real concern. The same would hold for accident investigations.[20] These simple changes, like the example cited above of a leader instilling the importance of safety by starting all meetings by discussing the safety issues, can do much to steer culture without much effort.

The second circumstance is the degree of participation. Members of an organization resist change when they perceive that it is foisted upon them. They are more receptive to change if they feel that they have been active participants in the implementation. They feel they have ownership in the process and are partners in the activities.[21] For changing cyber culture, an opportunity for participation is in the breakout of tasks in the strategies-to-tasks process described in Chapter 2. Senior leaders set out clear objectives and strategies (what to do), and the rest of the Air Force adapts its operations to achieve the objectives and strategies via tasks (how to do it).

### Provide Adequate Resources

Every initiative requires resources. Manpower effort will need to be redirected, and money will need to be allocated. During times of near-constant budgets, that will mean some other things will not get done. Members of the Air Force will notice the degree to which resources are allocated to a cultural shift in the attitudes toward cybersecurity. What leaders prioritize and fight for in the budget reflects their true priorities, regardless of what they say.[22] Members know that what gets funded drives what happens in the future. Talk and attention to cybersecurity will not move the culture substantially if it is not reflected in the budget. When a matter lacks budgetary prominence, members deduce that leaders do not really hold the matter to be important, and the members do not have the resources to follow up even if leaders did.

---

[19] Named after the process described in Technical Manual TO 00-25-107, *Maintenance Assistance*, Washington, D.C.: Secretary of the Air Force, August 15, 2011.

[20] The Navy did just this after several ship collisions and has now called for a cyber component as a routine part of incident investigations (Justin Katz, "Navy Cyber Team Investigating McCain Collision," *Inside Defense*, September 14, 2017; Amber Corrin, "Navy's New Weapon of Choice? Information," C4ISRNET website, February 7, 2018).

[21] Kets de Vries and Balazs, 1999.

[22] Mallak, 2001.

### Get Support External to the Air Force

Changing culture in the Air Force counter to the ambient culture in the rest of the DoD and government would be hard. Fortunately, in this case, there is at least the desire to see a better cyber culture in the organizations in which the Air Force is embedded. In fact, the other services, DoD, and the government writ large are also struggling with these changes. A clear plan and concerted effort in the Air Force could make the service an exemplar for other services (and beyond) and assist in securing the adequate resources.

### Drive the Changes into the Daily Routines of Members

If they are to be meaningful, the changes to cyber culture must become part of the routines of the members of the Air Force. Such changes emerge over time from a variety of driving forces. One such force is changes to policy and doctrine, such as our recommendation to rewrite AFPD 17-1. Another is to introduce cyber defensive and cyber resilient measures into tactics, techniques, and procedures; into technical orders; and into designed operational capability statements. Doing so introduces awareness into the daily routines of Air Force members and subjects them to accountability.

Policy changes form the foundation for wider ways of introducing the desired cyber cultural elements into personnel evaluation and promotion. Consideration of cybersecurity actions of members in awards and promotions reinforces the other actions. On the negative side, leaders could mention tolerance for poor cyber hygiene and have this influence their recommendations. On the positive side, leaders could cite individuals who have pointed out issues of concern or have contributed in a creative way to plan for how mission activities could be continued even in the event of a cyberattack.

### Pursue Comprehensive Change

Finally, Kets de Vries and Balazs note that any change needs to be comprehensive and integrated with other initiatives to avoid misalignment of incentives. Piecemeal policy changes will not suffice, as we argued in Chapter 2. The strategies-to-tasks framework we proposed in that chapter is a step toward a coherent, comprehensive effort that avoids strength in one area that is nullified by weakness in another.

Culture does not change overnight. Consistency of attention from leaders matters. Inconsistency of prioritized actions sends mixed messages to the members of the organization. If a leader pays close attention to one issue for a while, then another, followers often take the message that they are on their own to figure out which priority is most relevant to them.

Finally, a clear, common language binds an organization together to form a separate, coherent culture and helps integrate actions. A common language facilitates a common purpose. If members of the organization are debating what it means to be cyber resilient or what, exactly, cyberspace is, integration is disturbed, and an opportunity for common cause is diminished. This point reinforces the need for a clear objective and strategy for cybersecurity.

Although a shared language helps solidify a culture, a lot of jargon can isolate a subgroup from the rest of a community.[23] If those in cyber-specific organizations and cyber-specific career fields communicate with jargon and assumed knowledge that is not readily understood outside of a limited number of cyber aficionados, the tendency will be for that group to become isolated from the rest of the Air Force. That isolation will break a common culture across the enterprise.

We emphasize that all of these mechanisms need to percolate down from the top of leadership, be consistent across the Air Force, and persist over time.

---

[23] Mallak, 2001.

# 6. Conclusions and Recommendations

Although the topic of this report is enterprise-level management of cybersecurity and the associated assignment of roles and responsibilities, we would be remiss if we did not mention that none of the recommendations in this report will be effective if not properly resourced. Even with a carefully considered apportionment of roles and responsibilities, the level of money, manpower, or skills will constrain the ability to defend against and be resilient to adversary cyberspace operations. Several of the recommendations we make would require some additional resourcing. Given that the Air Force budget and manpower levels have remained relatively constant over the past decade, additional resources will probably have to come at the sacrifice of some other area of the Air Force.

## Objective and Strategy

Our principal recommendation is that the Air Force should issue a clearer objective and strategy for cybersecurity, embracing both cyber defensive measures and the ability to continue missions through adversary cyber operations in a holistic manner. We recommend that this guidance, perhaps issued by the Secretary of the Air Force as a revision of AFPD 17-1, set a single goal that all can understand their role in, list and assign the tasks to be done to fulfill the strategy more completely, specify how the tasks will be coordinated, and emphasize the ubiquitous presence of cyberspace and the universal role of every individual and organization in cybersecurity. The treatment of cybersecurity activities should employ a balance of cyber defensive measures and cyber resiliency measures (of systems and missions) and employ a balance of enterprise networks and cyber-physical systems. And the policy should clearly indicate that all individuals and organizations play a role in cybersecurity and that failure to perform that role effectively could be decisive.

## Task Allocation

We further recommend careful deliberation of the nature of these tasks. Activities that require quick decisions using detailed knowledge in a complex environment should be distinguished from those that do not. The advantages of placing the former activities into organizations with more decentralized structures and separating them from the latter should be balanced against any risks. Within the constraints of law and DoD regulations, this will raise issues about whether to separate tactical and strategic cybersecurity risk assessment and whether to separate the provisioning of enterprise network services from the cybersecurity of these services.

## Operational Risk

We recommend placing greater emphasis on operational risks and mission assurance (cyber resiliency) and that these be elevated to the same level as similar considerations for systems. An SRA would assess risks and propose mitigations on the system side, and an ORA would assess risk and propose mitigations on the operational side. We then recommend that the role of the authorizing official be adjusted to balance these two perspectives in accepting risk for the enterprise. All parties should be fed all relevant intelligence and test information. To perform these augmented duties, the authorizing official should be a dedicated position and not an additional duty placed on a senior official.

## Cybersecurity Integrity Program

To facilitate risk assessment at both the tactical and strategic levels, we recommend maintaining a cybersecurity integrity program for each system. This would be modeled after the aircraft structural integrity program. It would maintain a permanent record for the system for all relevant cybersecurity issues, including known threats, vulnerabilities, and any mitigations levied.

## Cultural Changes

Air Force members will need to make some decisions in cybersecurity that will not be codified in policy. Handling these situations effectively will require an appropriate cyberculture. The current culture is lacking, and leaders will need be the vanguards in changing it. They need to define a culture that, at minimum, includes the following:

- a sense that there is conflict in cyberspace between the United States and others that is ubiquitous in time and space
- a sense that operations in cyberspace might be decisive in warfare
- an understanding that all airmen, civilians, and contractors play a role in cybersecurity
- a realization that nothing can be completely secure in cyberspace that leads to a sense of personnel of their responsibility to carry on their mission(s) in the face of an attack through cyberspace
- a sense that connecting one system to another (or a network) carries potential risks
- a sense of obligation to report anomalies in data, nonnominal procedures, and potential cyber incidents.

The burden of changing this culture lies with leaders. Their actions will be more important than their words. Key actions would include paying attention to these cybersecurity matters, actively monitoring them, and making them true priorities consistently over time, including prioritizing them in the budget. The more passionate leaders are about these issues, the more it will help change the culture. Sanctions and rewards for individuals and units will bolster that message. To form a shared sense of reality, developing a common vocabulary that binds the Air

Force together in this common, integrated activity, rather than isolating cybersecurity to specialists, will also reinforce these messages. Eight actions would facilitate the change of culture:

- Persuade Air Force members that a cultural change is needed.
- Ensure the support and commitment of senior leadership and commanders for the changes.
- Present a clear and coherent plan for change.
- Build internal support for change and overcome any resistance.
- Provide adequate resources.
- Get support external to the Air Force.
- Drive the changes into the daily routines of members.
- Pursue the changes in a comprehensive manner.

These changes will not solve cybersecurity alone in the Air Force. But without clear direction at the enterprise level that identifies the full range of tasks needed for cybersecurity and apportions and coordinates them well, even well-executed actions by individuals and organizations risk being for naught as personnel leave gaps in their efforts and work in an uncoordinated way.

# References

AFI—*See* Air Force Instruction.

AFPD—*See* Air Force Policy Directive.

Air Force e-Publishing website, undated. As of October 31, 2019:
https://www.e-publishing.af.mil/Product-
Index/#/?view=org&orgID=10141&catID=1&isForm=false&modID=449&tabID=131

Air Force Instruction 17-101, *Risk Management Framework (RMF) for Air Force Information Technology*, Washington, D.C.: Department of the Air Force, February 2, 2017.

Air Force Instruction 63-101/20-101, *Integrated Life Cycle Management*, Washington, D.C.: Department of the Air Force, May 9, 2017.

Air Force Instruction 63-140, *Aircraft Structural Integrity Program*, Washington, D.C.: Department of the Air Force, April 7, 2014.

Air Force Instruction 91-202, *The US Air Force Mishap Prevention Program*, Washington, D.C.: Department of the Air Force, June 24, 2015, Change 1, February 15, 2017.

Air Force Policy Directive 17-1, *Cyberspace: Information Dominance Governance and Management*, Washington, D.C.: Department of the Air Force, April 12, 2016.

Air Force Policy Directive 17-2, *Cyberspace Operations*, Washington, D.C.: Department of the Air Force, April 12, 2016.

Alonso, Ricardo, Wouter Dessein, and Niko Matouschek, "Organizing to Adapt and Compete," *American Economic Journal: Microeconomics*, Vol. 7, No. 2, May 2015, pp.158–187.

Arthur, W. Brian, *The Nature of Technology: What It Is and How It Evolves*, New York: Free Press, 2009.

Ashibani, Yosef, and Qusay H. Mahmoud, "Cyber Physical Systems Security: Analysis, Challenges and Solutions," *Computers and Security*, Vol. 68, July 2017, pp. 81–97.

Bigley, Gregory A., and Karlene H. Roberts, "The Incident Command System: High-Reliability Organizing for Complex and Volatile Task Environments," *Academy of Management Journal*, Vol. 44, No. 6, December 2001, pp. 1281–1299.

Bitton, Ron, Andrey Finkelstein, Lior Sidi, Rami Puzis, Lior Rokach, and Asaf Shabtai, "Taxonomy of Mobile Users' Security Awareness," *Computers and Security*, Vol. 73, 2018, pp. 266–293.

Bodeau, Deborah, and Richard Graubart, *Cyber Resiliency Design Principles: Selective Use Throughout the Lifecycle in Conjunction With Related Disciplines*, Bedford, Mass.: MITRE Corporation, MTR170001, January 2017.

Brown, Allen E., and Gerald G. Grant, "Framing the Frameworks: A Review of IT Governance Research," *Communications of the Association for Information Systems*, Vol. 15, No. 38, May 2005, pp. 696–712.

Burton, Richard M., Børge Obel, and Dorthe Døjbak Håkonsson, *Organizational Design: A Step-by-Step Approach*, 3rd ed., Cambridge University Press, 2015.

Calvo, Guillermo A. and Stanislaw Wellisz, "Supervision, Loss of Control, and the Optimal Size of the Firm," *Journal of Political Economy*, Vol. 86, No. 5, October 1978, pp. 943–952.

CNSSI—*See* Committee on National Security Systems Instruction.

Coats, Jennifer C., and Frederick W. Rankin, "The Delegation of Decision Rights: An Experimental Investigation," in Marc J. Epstein and Mary A. Malina, eds., *Advances in Management Accounting*, Vol. 27, Bingley, U.K.: Emerald Group Publishing, 2016, pp. 39–71.

Colombo, Massimo G., and Marco Delmastro, "Delegation of Authority in Business Organizations: An Empirical Test," *Journal of Industrial Economics*, Vol. 52, No. 1, March 2004, pp. 53–80.

Committee on National Security Systems Instruction 1253, *Security Categorization and Control Selection for National Security Systems*, Committee on National Security Systems, March 27, 2014.

Committee on National Security Systems Instruction 4009, *Committee on National Security Systems (CNSS) Glossary*, Committee on National Security Systems, April 6, 2015.

Corrin, Amber, "Navy's New Weapon of Choice? Information," C4ISRNET website, February 7, 2018.

CrowdStrike, *2018 Global Threat Report: Blurring the Lines Between Statecraft and Tradecraft*, 2018.

Daft, Richard L., *Organization Theory and Design*, 9th ed., Mason, Ohio: Thomson South-Western, 2007.

Dalton, Dan R., William D. Todor, Michael J. Spendolini, Gordon J. Fielding, and Lyman W. Porter, "Organization Structure and Performance: A Critical Review," *Academy of Management Review*, Vol. 5, No. 1, January 1980, pp. 49–64.

Denford, James S., Gregory S. Dawson, and Kevin C. Desouza, "An Argument for Centralization of IT Governance in the Public Sector," presented at the 48th Hawaii International Conference on System Sciences, Kauai, Hawaii, 2015, pp. 4493–4501.

Denison, Daniel R., and Aneil K. Mishra, "Toward a Theory of Organizational Culture and Effectiveness," *Organization Science*, Vol. 6, No. 2, March–April 1995, pp. 204–223.

Department of Defense Directive 5205.02E, *DoD Operations Security (OPSEC) Program*, Department of Defense, June 20, 2012, Change 1, May 11, 2018.

Department of Defense Handbook MIL-HDBK-1785, *System Security Engineering Program Management Requirements*, Washington, D.C.: Department of Defense, August 1, 1995 (rescinded).

Department of Defense Instruction 8500.01, *Cybersecurity*, Department of Defense, March 14, 2014.

Department of Defense Instruction 8510.01, *Risk Management Framework (RMF) for DoD Information Technology (IT)*, Department of Defense, March 12, 2014, Change 2, July 28, 2017.

DoDI—See DoD Instruction

Earley, P. Christopher, Gregory B. Northcraft, Cynthia Lee, and Terri R. Lituchy, "Impact of Process and Outcome Feedback on the Relation of Goal Setting to Task Performance," *Academy of Management Journal*, Vol. 33, No. 1, March 1990, pp. 87–105.

Fernandez, Sergio, and Hal G. Rainey, "Managing Successful Organizational Change in the Public Sector," *Public Administration Review*, Vol. 66, No. 2, March–April 2006, pp. 168–176.

Ford, Robert C., and W. Alan Randolph, "Cross-Functional Structures: A Review and Integration of Matrix Organization and Project Management," *Journal of Management,* Vol. 18, No. 2, June 1992, pp. 267–294.

Freedman, Lawrence, *Strategy: A History*, New York: Oxford University Press, 2013.

Frost, Peter J., and Thomas A. Mahoney, "Goal Setting and the Task Process: I. An Interactive Influence on Individual Performance," *Organizational Behavior and Human Performance*, Vol. 17, No. 2, December 1976, pp. 328–350.

Gaim, Medhanie, Nils Wåhlin, Miguel Pina e Cunha, and Stewart Clegg, "Analyzing Competing Demands in Organizations: A Systematic Comparison," *Journal of Organization Design*, Vol. 7, No. 1, December 2018.

Galbraith, Jay R., *Designing Complex Organizations*, Reading, Mass.: Addison-Wesley, 1973.

Gosler, James and Lewis Von Thaer, *Resilient Military Systems and the Advanced Cyber Threat*, Washington, D.C.: U.S. Department of Defense, January 2013.

Hax, Arnoldo C., and Nicolas S. Majluf, "Organizational Design: A Survey and an Approach," *Operations Research*, Vol. 29, No. 3, May–June 1981, pp 417–447.

Hayashi, Yu-ichi, "State-of-the-Art Research on Electromagnetic Information Security," *Radio Science*, Vol. 51, No. 7, June 2016, pp. 1213–1219.

Hvistendahl, Mara, "3D Printers Vulnerable to Spying: Design Information Can Be Pilfered from the Sounds a Printer Makes," *Science*, Vol. 352, No. 6282, April 8, 2016, pp. 132–133.

Jensen, Michael C., and William H. Meckling, "Specific and General Knowledge, and Organizational Structure," in Lars Werin and Hans Wijkander, eds., *Contract Economics*, Oxford, U.K.: Blackwell, 1992, pp. 251–274.

Kahneman, Daniel, *Thinking, Fast and Slow*, New York: Farrar, Straus and Giroux, 2011.

Katz, Justin, "Navy Cyber Team Investigating McCain Collision," *Inside Defense*, September 14, 2017.

Kello, Lucas, *The Virtual Weapon and International Order*, New Haven, Conn.: Yale University Press, 2017.

Kent, Glenn A., *Concepts of Operations: A More Coherent Framework for Defense Planning*, Santa Monica, Calif.: RAND Corporation, N-2026-AF, 1983. As of September 4, 2019: https://www.rand.org/pubs/notes/N2026.html

Kent, Glenn A., *A Framework for Defense Planning*, Santa Monica, Calif.: RAND Corporation, R-3721-AF/OSD, 1989. As of September 4, 2019: https://www.rand.org/pubs/reports/R3721.html

Kent, Glenn A., with David Ochmanek, Michael Spirtas, and Bruce R. Pirnie, *Thinking About America's Defense: An Analytical Memoir*, Santa Monica, Calif.: RAND Corporation, OP-223-AF, 2008. As of September 4, 2019: https://www.rand.org/pubs/occasional_papers/OP223.html

Kernighan, Brian W., *Understanding the Digital World: What You Need to Know About Computers, the Internet, Privacy, and Security*, Princeton, N.J.: Princeton University Press, 2017.

Kets de Vries, Manfred F. R., and Katharina Balazs, "Transforming the Mind-Set of the Organization: A Clinical Perspective," *Administration & Society*, Vol. 30, No. 6, January 1999, pp. 640–675.

Klein, Gary, *Streetlights and Shadows: Searching for the Keys to Adaptive Decision Making*, Cambridge, Mass.: MIT Press, 2009.

Mallak, Larry, "Understanding and Changing Your Organization's Culture," *Industrial Management*, Vol. 43, No. 2, March–April 2001, pp. 18–24.

Malone, Thomas W., *The Future of Work: How the New Order of Business Will Shape Your Organization, Your Management Style and Your Life*, Boston, Mass.: Harvard Business School Press, 2004.

March, James G., Lee S. Sproull, and Michal Tamuz, "Learning From Samples of One or Fewer," *Organization Science*, Vol. 2, No. 1, February 1991, pp. 1–13.

Mintzberg, Henry, *The Structuring of Organizations: A Synthesis of Research*, Englewood Cliffs, N.J.: Prentice-Hall, 1979.

Monte, Matthew, *Network Attacks and Exploitation: A Framework*, Indianapolis, Ind.: John Wiley & Sons, 2015.

National Institute of Standards and Technology, *Guide for Applying the Risk Management Framework to Federal Information Systems: A Security Life Cycle Approach*, Washington, D.C.: U.S. Department of Commerce, NIST Special Publication 800-37, rev. 1, February 2010.

National Institute of Standards and Technology, *Security and Privacy Controls for Federal Information Systems and Organizations*, Washington, D.C.: U.S. Department of Commerce, NIST Special Publication 800-53, rev. 4, April 2013.

National Science Foundation, "Cyber-Physical Systems (CPS)," webpage, 2019. As of September 4, 2019:
https://www.nsf.gov/funding/pgm_summ.jsp?pims_id=503286

Nissim, Nir, Ran Yahalom, and Yuval Elovici, "USB-Based Attacks," *Computers and Security*, Vol. 70, September 2017, pp. 675–688.

NIST—*See* National Institute of Standards and Technology.

Pick, Roger Alan, "Shepherd or Servant: Centralization and Decentralization in Information Technology Governance," *International Journal of Management & Information Systems*, Vol. 19, No. 2, 2nd Qtr. 2015, pp. 61–68.

Public Law 104-106, National Defense Authorization Act for Fiscal Year 1996 (Divisions D and E), Section 5125, Clinger-Cohen Act of 1996.

Public Law 107-347, *Federal Information Security Management Act of 2002*, Title III of the *E-Government Act of 2002*, December 17, 2002.

Rajan, Raghuram G., and Julie Wulf, "The Flattening Firm: Evidence from Panel Data on the Changing Nature of Corporate Hierarchies," *Review of Economics and Statistics*, Vol. 88, No. 4, November 2006, pp. 759–773.

Ross, Lee, "The Intuitive Psychologist and His Shortcomings: Distortions in the Attribution Process," in Leonard Berkowitz, ed., *Advances in Experimental Social Psychology*, Vol. 10, New York: Academic Press, 1977, pp. 173–220.

Ross, Ron, Michael McEvilley, and Janet Carrier Oren, *Systems Security Engineering: Considerations for a Multidisciplinary Approach in the Engineering of Trustworthy Secure Systems*, Washington, D.C.: U.S. Department of Commerce, NIST Special Publication 800-160, November 2016.

Rumelt, Richard P., *Good Strategy, Bad Strategy: The Difference and Why It Matters*, New York: Crown Business, 2011.

Sagan, Scott D., *The Limits of Safety: Organizations, Accidents, and Nuclear Weapons*, Princeton, N.J.: Princeton University Press, 1993.

Schein, Edgar H., "Coming to a New Awareness of Organizational Culture," *Sloan Management Review*, Vol. 25, No. 2, Winter 1984, pp. 3–16.

Schein, Edgar H., and Peter Schein, *Organizational Culture and Leadership*, 5th ed., Hoboken, N.J.: John Wiley & Sons, 2017.

Schmidt, Lara, Caolionn O'Connell, Hirokazu Miyake, Akhil R. Shah, Joshua William Baron, Geof Nieboer, Rose Jourdan, David Senty, Zev Winkelman, Louise Taggart, Susanne Sondergaard, and Neil Robinson, *Cyber Practices: What Can the U.S. Air Force Learn From the Commercial Sector?* Santa Monica, Calif.: RAND Corporation, RR-847-AF, 2015. As of September 4, 2019:
https://www.rand.org/pubs/research_reports/RR847.html

Snyder, Don, Elizabeth Bodine-Baron, Mahyar A. Amouzegar, Kristin F. Lynch, Mary Lee, and John G. Drew, *Robust and Resilient Logistics Operations in a Degraded Information Environment*, Santa Monica, Calif.: RAND Corporation, RR-2015-AF, 2017. As of September 4, 2019:
https://www.rand.org/pubs/research_reports/RR2015.html

Snyder, Don, Bernard Fox, Kristin F. Lynch, Raymond E. Conley, John A. Ausink, Laura Werber, William Shelton, Sarah A. Nowak, Michael R. Thirtle, and Albert A. Robbert, *Assessment of the Air Force Materiel Command Reorganization: Report for Congress*, Santa Monica, Calif.: RAND Corporation, RR-389-AF, 2013. As of September 4, 2019:
https://www.rand.org/pubs/research_reports/RR389.html

Snyder, Don, Lauren A. Mayer, Guy Weichenberg, Danielle C. Tarraf, Bernard Fox, Myron Hura, Suzanne Genc, and Jonathan W. Welburn, *Measuring Cybersecurity and Cyber Resiliency*, Santa Monica, Calif.: RAND Corporation, RR-2703-AF, 2020. As of October 16, 2020:
https://www.rand.org/pubs/research_reports/RR2703.html

Snyder, Don, James D. Powers, Elizabeth Bodine-Baron, Bernard Fox, Lauren Kendrick, and Michael H. Powell, *Improving the Cybersecurity of U.S. Air Force Military Systems Throughout Their Life Cycles*, Santa Monica, Calif.: RAND Corporation, RR-1007-AF, 2015. As of September 5, 2019:
https://www.rand.org/pubs/research_reports/RR1007.html

von Solms, Basie, and Rossouw von Solms, "The 10 Deadly Sins of Information Security Management," *Computers and Security*, Vol. 23, No. 5 July 2004, pp. 371–376.

Steinbruner, John D., *The Cybernetic Theory of Decision*, Princeton, N.J.: Princeton University Press, 1974.

Technical Manual TO 00-25-107, *Maintenance Assistance*, Washington, D.C.: Secretary of the Air Force, August 15, 2011.

Thaler, David E., *Strategies to Tasks: A Framework for Linking Means and Ends*, Santa Monica, Calif.: RAND Corporation, MR-300-AF, 1993. As of September 5, 2019:
https://www.rand.org/pubs/monograph_reports/MR300.html

Thompson, Nik, Tanya Jane McGill, and Xuequn Wang, "'Security Begins at Home:' Determinants of Home Computer and Mobile Device Security Behavior," *Computers and Security*, Vol. 70, September 2017, pp. 376–391.

U.S.C.—*See* U.S. Code.

U.S. Code, Title 10, Armed Forces, Subtitle A, General Military Law, Part I, Organizational and General Military Powers, Chapter 4, Office of the Secretary of Defense, Section 131, Office of the Secretary of Defense.

U.S. Code, Title 10, Armed Forces, Subtitle A, General Military Law, Part I, Organizational and General Military Powers, Chapter 4, Office of the Secretary of Defense, Section 142, Chief Information Officer

U.S. Code, Title 10, Armed Forces, Subtitle A, General Military Law, Part IV, Service, Supply and Procurement, Chapter 131, Planning and Coordination, Section 2223, Information Technology: Additional Responsibilities of Chief Information Officers.

U.S. Code, Title 10, Armed Forces, Subtitle D, Air Force, Part I, Organization, Chapter 903, Department of the the Air Force, Section 9013, Secretary of the Air Force.

U.S. Code, Title 10, Armed Forces, Subtitle D, Air Force, Part I, Organization, Chapter 903, Department of the the Air Force, Section 9014, Office of the Secretary of the Air Force.

U.S. Code, Title 40, Public Buildings, Property, and Works, Subtitle III, Information Technology Management, Chapter 113, Responsibility for Acquisitions of Information Technology, Subchapter II, Executive Agencies, Section 11315, Agency Chief Information Officer.

da Veiga, Adéle, and Nico Martins, "Defining and Identifying Dominant Information Security Cultures and Subcultures," *Computers and Security*, Vol. 70, September 2017, pp. 72–94.

Vu Pham, Dung, Ali Syed, and Malka N. Halgamuge, "Universal Serial Bus Based Software Attacks and Protection Solutions," *Digital Investigation*, Vol. 7, April 2011, pp. 172–184.

Williamson, Oliver E., "Hierarchical Control and Optimum Firm Size," *Journal of Political Economy*, Vol. 75, No. 2, April 1967, pp. 123–138.